P9-ELG-193

RON FRY'S **HOW TO STUDY** PROGRAM

IMPROVE YOUR READING

FOURTH EDITION

BY RON FRY

CAREER
PRESS
Franklin Lakes, NJ

IMPROVE YOUR READING, 4TH EDITION
Cover design by Design Solutions
Printed in the U.S.A. by Book-mart Press

To order this title, please call toll-free 1-800-CAREER-1 (NJ
and Canada: 201-848-0310) to order using VISA or MasterCard,
or for further information on books from Career Press.

The Career Press, Inc., 3 Tice Road, PO Box 687,
Franklin Lakes, NJ 07417
www.careerpress.com

Library of Congress Cataloging-in-Publication Data

Fry, Ronald W.
    Improve your reading / by Ron Fry. — 4th ed.
        p.   cm.
    Includes index.
    ISBN 1-56414-458-5 (paper)
    1. Reading. 2. Reading comprehension.   I. Title.

LB1050 .F797 2000
428.4 — dc21   00-031195

Contents

IMPROVE
YOUR
READING

Read On!

HIS YEAR MARKS another major milestone in the decade-long evolution of my *How to Study Program* — the reissuance of new editions of the key volumes: *How to Study* itself, now in a fifth edition; fourth editions of *Improve Your Memory, Improve Your Reading, Improve Your Writing,* and *"Ace" Any Test;* and a second edition of *Get Organized. (Take Notes, Manage Your Time,* and *Use Your Computer,* though still available, were not revised this year.)

I am truly proud, though somewhat amazed, that *How to Study* itself is now well into its second decade. While all authors want to believe their books will last forever, most wind up in the remainder bin far sooner than we would ever like (or admit).

Why are these books the best-selling series of study guides ever published? Why are they still so *needed*, not only by students but by their parents, who want so badly for their children to do well? Because virtually all of the conditions I've been writing and speaking about across the country since 1988 have remained...or gotten *worse:*

1. Despite modest recent improvements in test scores, U.S. students still score abysmally low compared to students in many other countries, especially on science and math tests.

2. Most parents, when polled, say improving our public schools is our nation's number one priority. Those same parents do *not* think public schools are doing a very good job teaching their kids much of anything.

3. Business leaders continue to complain that far too many entry-level job candidates can barely read, write, add, or multiply. Many can't fill out job applications! As a result, businesses are spending billions to teach employees the basic skills everyone agrees they should have learned in school.

It's almost inevitable that these conditions will *continue to worsen*. This means that the old problems that most affect students' ability to learn—overcrowded classrooms, lack of resources (especially computers and other new technologies), lack of qualified teachers—will continue to frustrate those who want to learn but need help.

As a result, the need for my books will, unfortunately, continue, because they offer exactly the help students need and their parents demand.

So who are you?

A number of you are students, not just the high school students I always thought were my readers, but also college students (a rousing plug for their high school preparation) and _junior_ high school students (which says something far more positive about their motivation and eventual success).

Many of you reading this are adults. Some of you are returning to school, and some of you are long out of school but have figured out that if you could learn _now_ the study skills your teachers never taught you, you'd do better in your careers—especially if you were able to read faster...and retain what you read better and longer.

All too many of you are parents with the same lament: "How do I get Johnny to do better in school? He thinks _Calvin and Hobbes_ is the height of literature."

I want to briefly take the time to address every one of the audiences for this book and discuss some of the factors particular to each of you:

If you're a high school student

You should be particularly comfortable with both the language and format of this book—its relatively short sentences and paragraphs, occasionally humorous (hopefully) headings and subheadings, and a reasonable but certainly not outrageous vocabulary. I wrote it with you in mind!

If you're a junior high school student

I doubt you'll have trouble with the concepts or language in this book. Sixth, seventh, and eighth grade is the perfect time to learn the different ways to read and the methods to better retain whatever you're reading. You're probably just discovering that _The Baby-sitters Club_ series is _not_ what your parents or teachers had in mind when they encouraged you to read "the classics."

If you're a "traditional" college student...

...somewhere in the 18 to 25 age range, I would have hoped you had already mastered most, if not all, of the basic study skills, especially reading and writing. Since you haven't, please make learning, using, and mastering all of the study skills covered in my *How to Study Program* an absolute priority.

Do not pass "Go." Do not go on a date. Take the time to learn these skills now. You may have been able to kid yourself that mediocre or even poor reading skills didn't stop you from finishing, perhaps even succeeding in, high school. I guarantee you will not be able to kid *anyone* in college. You must master all of the skills in this book to survive, let alone succeed.

If you're the parent of a student of any age

Your child's school is probably doing little if anything to teach him or her how to study. Which means he or she is not learning how to *learn*. And that means he or she is not learning how to *succeed*.

Should the schools be accomplishing that? Absolutely. After all, we spend $275 billion on elementary and secondary education in this country, *an average of $6,000 per student per year*.

We ought to be getting more for that money than possible graduation, some football cheers, and a diploma to hang on the wall.

What can parents do?

There are probably even more dedicated parents out there than dedicated students, because the first phone call at any of my radio or TV appearances usually comes from a sincere and worried parent asking, "What can I do to help my kid do better in school?" Okay, here they are, the rules for parents of students of any age:

1. **Set up a homework area.** Free of distraction, well-lit, all necessary supplies handy.

2. **Set up a homework routine.** When and where it gets done. Same time, same place, every day.

3. **Set homework priorities.** Actually, just make the point that homework *is* the priority — before a date, before TV, before going out to play, before whatever.

4. **Make reading a habit** — for them, certainly, but also for you, presuming it isn't already. Kids will inevitably do what you *do*, not what you *say* (even if you say *not* to do what you *do*). So if you keep nagging them to read while *you* turn on the eighth sitcom of the night, what message do you think you're giving them?

5. **Turn off the TV.** Or, at the very least, severely limit when and how much TV-watching is appropriate. This may be the toughest one. Believe me, I'm the father of an 11-year-old. I know. Do your best.

6. **Talk to the teachers.** Find out what your kids are supposed to be learning. If you don't, you can't really supervise. You might even be teaching them things at odds with what the teacher's trying to do.

7. **Encourage and motivate**, but don't nag them to do their homework. It doesn't work.

8. **Supervise their work**, but don't fall into the trap of *doing* their homework for them.

9. **Praise them to succeed**, but don't overpraise them for mediocre work. Kids know when you're slinging it. Be wary of any school or

teacher that is more worried about your kid's "self-esteem" than her grades, skills, and abilities. I'm not advocating the withdrawal of kudos for good work, but kids need to get the message that "you get what you pay for"; that you need to work hard to actually *earn* rewards. Horror stories about teachers giving out good grades, reducing standards, or not assigning homework because they're afraid some of the kids will "feel bad" if they don't do well are exactly that—horrible, scary stories. Such tactics merely set kids up for *bigger* failures down the road in a world that will place a premium on your skills and abilities and not care how they "feel" about it.

10. **Convince them of reality.** (This is for older students.) Okay, I'll admit it's almost as much of a stretch as turning off the TV, but learning and believing that the real world will not care about their grades but measure them solely by what they know and what they can do is a lesson that will save many tears (probably yours). It's probably never too early to (carefully) let your boy or girl genius get the message that life is not fair. Which is why teaching them resilience and determination—so they'll pick themselves up, dust themselves off, and try again when they fail— is paramount.

11. **If you can afford it, get your kid(s) a computer** and all the software they can handle. Many people have been saying it for years (including me) and there really is no avoiding it: Your kids, whatever their age, absolutely must master technology (computers) in order to survive, let alone succeed, in school and after school. There's even new empirical data to back up all the braying:

A recent decade-long study has shown that kids who master computers learn faster and earn higher test scores.

12. **Turn off the TV already!**
13. **Get wired.** The Internet is the greatest invention of our age and an unbelievable tool for students of any age. While it's impossible to list even a smattering of helpful sites in a book this brief, parents of elementary and high school students should check out the following:

> *www.schoolwork.org*
> *www.sunsite.berkeley.edu/KidsClick*
> *www.HomeworkCentral.com*
> (a division of *www.bigchalk.com*)
> *www.iln.net*
> *www.tutor.com*

The importance of your involvement

Don't for a minute underestimate the importance of *your* commitment to your child's success: Your involvement in your child's education is absolutely essential to his or her eventual success. The results of every study done in the last three decades about what affects a child's success in school demonstrate that only one factor *overwhelmingly* affects it, every time: parental involvement. Not the size of the school, the money spent per pupil, the number of language labs, how many of the students go on to college, how many great teachers there are (or lousy ones). All factors, yes. *But none as significant as the effect you can have.*

So please, take the time to read this book yourself (and all of the others in the series, but especially **How to Study**). Learn what your kids *should* be learning (and which of the other subject-specific books in the series your child needs the most).

You can help tremendously, *even if you were not a great student yourself, even if you never learned great study skills.* You can learn now with your child — it will help her in school, and it'll help *you* on the job, whatever your field.

If you're a nontraditional student

If you're going back to high school, college, or graduate school at age 25, 45, 65, or 85 — you probably need the help my books offer more than anyone! As much as I emphasize that it's rarely too early to learn good study habits, I must also emphasize that it's never too *late*.

If you're returning to school and attempting to carry even a partial load of courses while simultaneously holding down a job, raising a family, or both, there are some particular problems you face that you probably didn't the first time you were in school:

Time and money pressures. Let's face it, when all you had to worry about was going to school, it simply *had* to be easier than going to school, raising a family, and working for a living simultaneously. (And it was!) Mastering all of the techniques of time management is even more essential if you are to effectively balance your many responsibilities to your career, family, clubs, friends, and so forth, with your commitment to school. Money management may well be another essential skill, whether figuring out how to pay for childcare (something you probably didn't have to worry about the last time you were in school) or how to manage all your responsibilities while cutting your hours at work to make time for school.

Self-imposed fears of inadequacy. You may well convince yourself that you're just "out of practice" with all this school stuff. You don't even remember what to do with a highlighter! While some of this fear is valid, most is not. The valid part is that you are returning to an academic atmosphere, one that you may not have visited for a decade or two. And it *is* different (which I'll discuss more later on) than the "work-a-day" world. That's just a matter of adjustment and, trust me, it will take a matter of days, if not hours, to dissipate. I suspect what many of you are really fearing is that you just aren't in that school "mentality" anymore, that you don't "think" the same way. Or, perhaps more pertinent to this book, that the skills you need to succeed in school are rusty.

I think these last fears are groundless. You've been out there thinking and doing for quite a few years, perhaps very successfully, so it's really ridiculous to think school will be so different. It won't be. Relax. And while you may think your study skills are rusty, as we discussed earlier, you've probably been using them every day in your career. Even if I can't convince you, you have my *How to Study Program*, your refresher course. It will probably teach you more about studying than you ever forgot.

Maybe you're worried because you didn't exactly light up the academic power plant the first time around. Well, neither did Edison or Einstein or a host of other relatively successful people. But then, you've changed rather significantly since then, haven't you? Held a series of jobs, raised a family, saved money, taken on more and more responsibility? Concentrate on how much *more* qualified you are for school now than you were then!

Feeling you're "out of your element." This is a slightly different fear, the fear that you just don't fit in any more. After all, you're not 18 again. But then, neither are fully half the college students on campuses today. That's right, fully 50 percent of all college students are older than 25. The reality is, you'll probably feel more in your element now than you did the first time around!

You'll see teachers differently. Probably a plus. It's doubtful you'll have the same awe you did the first time around. At worst, you'll consider teachers your equals. At best, you'll consider them younger and not necessarily as successful or experienced as you are. In either event, you probably won't be quite as ready to treat your college professors as if they were akin to some deity.

There *are* differences in academic life. It's slower than the "real" world, and you may well be moving significantly faster than its normal pace. When you were 18, an afternoon without classes meant a game of Frisbee. Now it might mean catching up on a week's worth of errands, cooking (and freezing) a week's worth of dinners, and/or writing four reports due last week. Despite your own hectic schedule, do not expect campus life to accelerate in response. You will have to get used to people and systems with far less interest in speed.

Some random thoughts about learning

Learning shouldn't be painful and certainly doesn't have to be boring, though it's far too often both. However, it's not necessarily going to be wonderful and painless, either. Sometimes you actually have to work hard to figure something out or get a project done. That *is* reality.

It's also reality that everything isn't readily apparent or easily understandable. Tell yourself that's okay and learn to get past it. Heck, if you think you should understand everything you read the first time through, you're kidding yourself. Learning something slowly doesn't mean there's anything wrong with you. It may be a subject that virtually everybody learns slowly.

A good student doesn't panic when something doesn't seem to be getting through. He just takes his time, follows whatever steps apply, and remains confident that the light bulb will inevitably go on.

Parents often ask me, "How can I motivate my teenager?" My initial response is usually to smile and say, "If I knew the answer to that question, I would have retired very wealthy quite some time ago." However, I think there _is_ an answer, but it's not something _parents_ can do—it's something you, the student, have to decide: Are you going to spend the school day interested and alert or bored and resentful?

It's really that simple. Why not develop the attitude that you have to go to school anyway, so rather than being bored or miserable while you're there, you might as well be active and learn as much as possible? The difference between a C and an A or B for many students is, I firmly believe, merely a matter of wanting to do better. As I constantly stress in interviews, inevitably you will leave school. And very quickly, you'll discover the premium is on what you know and what you can do. Grades won't count anymore, and neither will tests. So you can learn it all now or regret it later.

How many times have you said to yourself, "I don't know why I'm bothering trying to learn this calculus (or algebra, geometry, physics, chemistry, history, whatever). I'll _never_ use this again!"? I hate to burst bubbles, but unless you've got a patent on some great new fortune-telling device, you have _no clue_ what you're going to need to know tomorrow or next week, let alone next year or in a decade.

I've been amazed in my own life how things I did with no specific purpose in mind (except probably to earn money) turned out years later to be not just invaluable to my life or career but essential. How was I to know when I took German as my language elective in high school that the most important international trade show in book publishing, my field, was in Frankfurt...Germany? Or that the basic skills I learned one year working for an accountant (while I was writing my first book) would become essential when I later started four companies? Or how important basic math skills would be in selling and negotiating over the years? (Okay, I'll admit it: I haven't used a differential equation in 20 years, but, hey, you never know!)

So learn it *all*. And don't be surprised if the subject you'd vote "least likely to ever be useful" winds up being the key to your fame and fortune.

There *are* other study guides

Though I immodestly maintain my *How to Study Program* to be the most helpful to the most people, there are certainly lots of other purported study books out there. Unfortunately, I don't think many of them deliver what they promise. In fact, I'm actually getting mad at the growing number of study guides out there claiming to be "the sure way to straight A's" or something of the sort. These are also the books that dismiss reasonable alternative ways to study and learn with, "Well, that never worked for me," as if that is a valid reason to dismiss it, as if we should *care* that it didn't work for the author.

Inevitably, these other books promote the authors' "system," which usually means what *they* did to get through school. This "system," whether basic and traditional or wildly quirky, may or may not work for you. So what do you do if "their" way of taking notes makes no sense to you? Or you master their highfalutin "Super Student Study Symbols" and still get C's?

I'm not getting into a Dennis Miller rant here, but there are very few "rights" and "wrongs" out there in the study world. There's certainly no single "right" way to attack a multiple-choice test or absolute "right" way to take notes. So don't get fooled into thinking there *is*, especially if what you're doing seems to be working for you. Don't change what "ain't broke" just because some self-proclaimed study guru claims what you're doing is all wet. Maybe he's all wet. After all, if his system works for you, all it *really* means is that you have the same likes, dislikes, talents, or skills as he does.

Needless to say, don't read _my_ books looking for the Truth—that single, inestimable system of "rules" that works for everyone. You won't find it, 'cause there's no such bird. You _will_ find a plethora of techniques, tips, tricks, gimmicks, and what-have-you, some or all of which may work for you, some of which won't. Pick and choose, change and adapt, figure out what works for you. Because _you_ are the one responsible for creating _your_ study system, _not me._

Yes, I'll occasionally point out "my way" of doing something. I may even suggest that I think it offers some clear advantages to all the alternative ways of accomplishing the same thing. That _doesn't_ mean it's some carved-in-stone, deviate-from-the-sacred-Ron-Fry-study-path-under-penalty-of-a-writhing-death kind of rule.

I've used the phrase "study smarter, not harder" as a sort of catch phrase in promotion and publicity for the _How to Study Program_ for more than a decade. So what does it mean to you? Does it mean I guarantee you'll spend less time studying? Or that the least amount of time is best? Or that studying isn't ever supposed to be difficult?

Hardly. It does mean that studying inefficiently is wasting time that could be spent doing other (okay, probably more _fun_) things and that getting your studying done as quickly and efficiently as possible is a realistic, worthy, and _attainable_ goal. I'm no stranger to hard work, but I'm not a monastic dropout who thrives on self-flagellation. I try not to work harder than I have to!

www.study.com

In 1988, when I wrote the first edition of _How to Study_, I composed it, formatted it, and printed it on (gasp) a personal computer. Yes, boys and girls, in those halycon days, I was surfing a wave that didn't hit shore for a few more years. Most people did _not_ have a computer, yet alone a neighborhood network and DSL, or surf the Web (whatever that was), or chat online, or Instant Message their friends, or...you get the point.

In case you've been living in a cave that Bill Gates forgot to wire, those days are very dead and gone. And you should cheer, even if you aren't sure what DOS was (is? could be?). Because the spread of the personal computer and, even more, the Internet, has taken studying from the Dark Ages to the Info Age in merely a decade.

As a result, you will find all of my books assume you have a computer and know how to use it — for note-taking, reading, writing papers, researching, and much more. There are many tasks that may be harder on a computer — and I'll point them out — but don't believe for a second that a computer won't help you tremendously, whatever your age, whatever your grades.

As for the Internet, it has absolutely revolutionized research. Whether you're writing a paper, putting together a reading list, studying for the SAT, or just trying to organize your life, it has become a more valuable tool than the greatest library in the world. Heck, it *is* the greatest library in the world...and more. So if you aren't Internet savvy (yes, I'm talking to the parents out there, couldn't you tell?), admit you're a dummy, get a book (over the Internet, of course), and get wired. You'll be missing far too much — and be studying far harder — without it.

In case you were wondering

Before we get on with all the tips and techniques necessary to read better and with more comprehension, let me make two important points about all of my study books.

First, I believe in gender equality, in writing as well as in life. Unfortunately, I find constructions such as "he and she," "s/he," "womyn," and other such stretches to be some-times painfully awkward. I have therefore attempted to sprinkle pronouns of both genders throughout the text.

Second, you will find many pieces of advice, lists, ex-amples, phrases, and sections spread throughout two or more of the books in my *How to Study Program*. Certainly *How to Study*, which is an overview of all the study skills, necessarily contains, though in summarized form, some of each of my other books.

The repetition is unavoidable. While I urge everyone to read all of the books in the series, but especially *How to Study*, they *are* nine individual books. And many people only buy one of them. Consequently, I must include in each the pertinent material *for that topic*, even if that material is then repeated in a second or even a third book.

That said, I can guarantee that the nearly 1,200 pages of my *How to Study Program* contain the most wide-ranging, comprehensive, and complete system of studying ever pub-lished. I have attempted to create a system that is usable, that is useful, that is practical, that is learnable. One that *you* can use—whatever your age, whatever your level of achieve-ment, whatever your IQ—to start doing better in school, in work, and in life *immediately*.

—Ron Fry
May 2000

CHAPTER 1

Reading: The Mother of All Study Skills

 THINK YOU'LL find this book unlike any you've read before. If you take the time to read it, I promise it will make everything else you have to read — whatever your student status, whatever your job, whatever your age — a lot easier to get through.

Why? Because I'm going to show you how to plow through *all* your reading assignments — whatever the subjects — better and faster...*and* how to remember *more* of what you read.

This book is *not* a gimmicky speed-reading method. It's not a spelling and grammar guide. Nor is it a lecture on the joys of reading. It's a *practical* guide, geared to *you* — a student of any age who isn't necessarily a poor reader, but who wants to get more from reading and do better in school and in life.

Personally, I love to read: the classics, spy thrillers, sports magazines, the newspaper, the back of the cereal box. When bored, tired, relaxing, or eating, I'll read just about anything handy, just to be able to read *some*thing.

But, believe me, just because I loved to read didn't mean it was easy for me to face some of those deadly textbook reading assignments. As a student, you inevitably will be required, as I was, to spend hours poring through ponderous, fact-filled, convoluted reading assignments for subjects that are required but not exactly up there on the "All-Time Favorites" list.

You may love reading for pleasure but have trouble reading textbook assignments for certain subjects. You may get the reading done but forget what you've read nearly as quickly as you read it. Or you just may hate the thought of sitting still to read *anything*. What*ever* kind of student you are—and whatever your level of reading skill—I've written this book to help you surmount your reading challenge, *whatever it may be.*

And that includes, for those of you long out of school, reading those nap-inducing business tomes, trade magazine articles, and other work-related stuff that's rarely reader-friendly.

You'll learn what you *should* read—and what you don't *have* to. You'll discover how to reduce the time you spend reading, how to identify the main idea in your reading, as well as the important details, and how to remember more of what you read.

I'll show you different ways to read various types of books, from dry science texts to cumbersome classics.

Who knows? I might even convince you reading is fun!

When you're a *good* reader, the world is your oyster—you qualify for better schools, better jobs, better pay. Poor readers qualify for poor jobs and less-fulfilling lives.

Ready to begin? Get motivated!

Any attempt to improve your reading must begin with motivation. Reading is not a genetic trait that is written in your DNA—there's no gene that makes you a good or bad reader like the ones that decide your hair or eye color. For the most part, reading is an *acquired* skill. A skill *you* can secure, grow, and sharpen. You just have to *want* to.

Within this book, I will address a number of very practical techniques that are sure to increase your reading comprehension. But they are just *techniques.*

You'll invariably find them utterly useless if you are not motivated to read in the first place.

As the Nike commercial lambastes all of us weekend warriors—"Just Do It!" This attitude—not technique—is where the quest for improved reading begins. You must make reading a habit.

Good reader vs. poor reader

Look at the following comparison of a good reader and a poor reader as if you were some corporate hotshot who could hire just one of the individuals:

Good reader: You read for purpose. You've clearly defined your reason for reading—a question you want answered, facts you must remember, ideas you need to grasp, current events that affect you, or just the pleasure of following a well-written story.

Poor reader: Yes, you read, but often have no real reason for doing so. You aimlessly struggle through assigned reading, with little effort to grasp the "message."

Good reader: You read and assimilate thought. You hear and digest the concepts and ideas communicated.

Poor reader: You get lost in the muddle of words, struggling to make sense of what the author is trying to say. You are often bored because you force yourself to read every word to "get the message"...which you don't.

Good reader: You read critically and ask questions to evaluate whether the author's arguments are reasonable or off-the-wall. You recognize biases and don't just "believe" everything you read.

Poor reader: You swallow everything you read — hook, line, and sinker. You suffer from the delusion that everything in print is true, and you are easily diverted from what you formerly believed to be true by any argument that sounds good.

Good reader: You read a variety of books, magazines, and newspapers — not limiting your reading to a *Far Side* humor book. You enjoy all types of reading — fiction, poetry, biography, current events.

Poor reader: You're a one-track reader — you read the sports pages, comics, or Gothic novels. Current events? You catch updates about your world from occasional TV news "sound bites."

Good reader: You enjoy reading and embrace it as an essential tool in your effort to better yourself.

Poor reader: You hate to read, deeming it a chore to be endured only when you have to. Reading is "boring."

Take a minute and ask yourself, who would *you* hire? Yes, you might hire Mr. Poor Reader...in some low-paying job. But would you ever put someone with such low-level reading skills in a responsible position?

At this point, I won't ask you to evaluate your own level of reading skills. Characterizing yourself as a "good" or "poor" reader was not the point of this exercise. What is important is to realize that Ms. Good Reader didn't spring full-blown from Zeus's cranium reading Shakespearean sonnets and quoting Winston Churchill. She learned to read the same way you and I did.

In time and through making reading a habit, Ms. Good Reader acquired and honed a skill that will open a world of opportunity to her.

Mr. Poor Reader, at some point, decided that being a good reader was not worth the effort and made *poor* reading his habit.

The good news is that being a poor reader is not a life sentence — you *can* improve your reading. The challenge is to find the motivation!

How fast can you understand?

When we read too fast or too slowly, we understand nothing.

–Pascal

Are you worried that you read too slowly? You probably shouldn't be — less-rapid readers are not necessarily less able. What counts is what you comprehend and remember. And like anything else, practice will probably increase your speed levels. If you must have a ranking, read the 300-word selection below from start to finish, noting the elapsed time on your watch. Score yourself as follows:

Less than 30 seconds	very fast
31-45 seconds	fast
46-60 seconds	high average
61-89 seconds	average
90-119 seconds	slow
120 seconds or more	very slow

Abdollah Nouri does not look like a dangerous counter-revolutionary. In a nation run by clerics, he ranks among the most senior, not quite an ayatullah but a *hojatolislam*, or "proof of Islam." His outspokenness is one reason the powers that be in Iran wish to destroy him.

This week Nouri will be called before a court to answer a 44-page indictment. He stands accused of dishonoring the Ayatullah Khomeini, undermining the authority of Iran's ruling clergy, and promoting relations with the U.S. If he is convicted, he faces a hefty fine, lashes of the whip, or a dozen years in prison. Much more critically, Nouri will then be disqualified from heading the reform ticket in next February's elections, thus ending any chance of his becoming the powerful speaker of Iran's 270-seat parliament, the Majlis-e-Shura. A victory by Nouri is crucial to his chief ally, the embattled reformist President of Iran, Mohammed Khatami, and his efforts to promote moderation, expand freedom, and normalize Iran's relations with the outside world.

This is not Nouri's first scuffle with hard-liners: In an impeachment trial last year, parliament ousted him as Minister of the Interior for permitting student demonstrations. Since then, his main vehicle of dissent has been the national daily *Khordad*. The newspaper has published antiregime opinions by prominent clerics, notably Grand Ayatullah Hossein Ali Montazeri, who has been under house arrest since 1997 for questioning *velayat-e-faqih*, the absolute authority of the clergy.

Being the patron and publisher of such notions has made Nouri one of the most popular politicians in Iran. [Khatami's] strategy is to send a flood of loyalist candidates to the election board, so that even if political stars like Nouri are barred, a solid number will survive the vetting process and get elected. Nouri praises Khatami for making government more accountable but warns that the President's program will face "serious problems" if reform forces are unfairly excluded from the next parliament.

Now answer the following questions *without referring back to the text*:

1. Nouri's chief ally is ___.
   a. the Ayatullah Khomeini
   b. the parliament
   c. Iran's president
   d. the *Khordad*

2. Nouri's main vehicle of dissent since his impeachment trial has been ___.
   a. the Ayatullah Khomeini
   b. the Majlis-e-Shura, Iran's parliament
   c. Mohammed Khatami, Iran's president
   d. the *Khordad*, the national daily newspaper

3. Which of the following has Nouri not been indicted for?
   a. undermining the authority of Iran's ruling clergy
   b. conspiring a government takeover
   c. promoting relations with the United States
   d. dishonoring the Ayatullah Khomeini

4. Iran's 270-seat parliament is called the ___.
   a. *Khordad*
   b. Ayatullah Khomeini
   c. Majlis-e-Shura
   d. *hojatolislam*

A good reader should be reading fast or very fast and have gotten at least three of the four questions correct.

You should only worry — and plan to do something about it — if you fall in the slow or very slow range and/or missed two or more questions. Otherwise, you are probably reading as fast as you need to and retaining most of what you read.

Again, the relationship between speed and comprehension is paramount: Read *too* fast and you may comprehend *less*; reading more slowly does not necessarily mean you're not grasping the material.

What decreases reading speed/comprehension:

1. Reading aloud or moving your lips when you read.
2. Reading mechanically — using your finger to follow words, moving your head as you read.
3. Applying the wrong *kind* of reading to the material.
4. Lacking sufficient vocabulary.

There are several things you can do to improve these reading mechanics.

To increase your reading speed:

1. Focus your attention and concentration.
2. Eliminate outside distractions.
3. Provide for an uncluttered and comfortable environment.
4. Don't get hung up on single words or sentences, but *do* look up (in the dictionary) key words that you must understand in order to grasp an entire concept.
5. Try to grasp overall concepts rather than attempting to understand every detail.
6. If you find yourself moving your lips when you read (vocalization), practice reading with a pen or some other (non-toxic, non-sugary) object in your mouth. If it falls out while you're reading, you know you have to keep working!

To increase comprehension:

1. Try to make the act of learning sequential—comprehension is built by adding new knowledge to existing knowledge.
2. Review and rethink at designated points in your reading. Test yourself to see if the importance of the material is getting through.
3. If things don't add up, discard your conclusions. Go back, reread, and try to find an alternate conclusion.
4. Summarize what you've read, rephrasing it in your notes, in your own words.

Most importantly, read at the speed that's comfortable for you. Though I *can* read extremely fast, I *choose* to read novels much more slowly so I can appreciate the authors' word play. Likewise, any material that I find particularly difficult to grasp slows me right down. I read newspapers, popular magazines, and the like very fast, seeking to grasp the information but not worrying about every detail.

Should you take some sort of speed reading course, especially if your current speed level is low?

Reading for speed has some merit—many people who are slow readers read as little as possible, simply because they find it so tedious and boring. But just reading faster is not the answer to becoming a good reader.

I can't see that such a course could particularly *hurt* you in any way. I can also, however, recommend that you simply keep practicing reading, which will increase your speed naturally.

Don't remember less...faster

Retention is primarily a product of what you understand. It has little to do with how *fast* you read, how great an outline you can construct, or how many fluorescent colors you can use to mark your textbooks. Reading a text, grasping the message, and remembering it are the fundamentals that make for high-level retention. Reading at a 1,000-word-per-minute clip does not necessarily mean that you have a clue as to what a text really says.

As you work toward improving your reading, realize that speed is secondary to comprehension. If you can read an assignment faster than anyone in class, but can't give a one-sentence synopsis of what you read, you lose. If you really get the author's message—even if it takes you an hour or two longer than some of your friends—your time will pay off in huge dividends in class and later in life.

That's why this book concentrates only on how you as a student can increase what you retain from your reading assignments. Whether you're reading a convoluted textbook that bores even the professor to tears or a magazine article, newspaper feature, or novel, you follow a certain process to absorb what you've read, which consists of:

1. Grasping the main idea.
2. Gathering the facts.
3. Figuring out the sequence of events.
4. Drawing conclusions.

When you spend an hour reading an assignment and then can't recall what you've just read, it's usually because a link in this chain has been broken. You've skipped one of these crucial steps in your reading process, leaving your understanding of the material filled with gaps.

To increase your retention rate, you need to master *each level* in this chain of comprehension. Not everything you read will require that you comprehend on all four levels. Following a set of cooking directions, for example, simply requires that you discern the sequence for adding all ingredients. Other reading will demand that you are able to compile facts, identify a thesis, and give some critical thought to its validity.

Ms. Good Reader is not only able to perform at each level of comprehension, but also has developed an instinct: She recognizes that certain things she reads can be read *just* to gather facts or *just* to grasp the main idea. She then is able to read quickly to accomplish this goal and move on to her next assignment — or to that Stephen King novel she's been dying to read.

This book will help you develop a sense of what is involved in *each* step of the reading process.

The first chapters will address these different steps and provide exercises designed to help you master each stage in the process of retaining what you read.

In the final chapters, we will look at how to read literature, how to read a math or science textbook, and how to outline so that you can easily review a text.

By the time you finish this short book, you should find that by following the procedures I've suggested, you have significantly improved your reading comprehension.

Finding other textbooks

Few textbooks are written by what most of us would even remotely call professional writers. While the authors and editors might well be experts, even legends, in a particular subject, writing in jargon-free, easy-to-grasp prose is probably not their strong suit. You will occasionally be assigned a textbook that is so obtuse you aren't even sure whether to read it front to back, upside down, or inside out.

If you find a particular chapter, section, or entire textbook as tough to read as getting your baby brother to do you a favor, get to the library or a bookstore and find *another* book covering the *same* subject area that you *can* understand. You might even consider asking your teacher or professor for recommendations. He or she will probably make your job of finding a *readable* text a lot easier. You may even score some brownie points for your seeming initiative (as long as you don't wonder aloud what caused him or her to select that torturous text in the first place!).

"Ron," I hear you grumbling, "what happened to the 'study smarter, not harder' bit? This can't *possibly* be a time-saver. Heck, I'll bet the books don't even cover the subject in the same way, let alone follow the same sequence! I'll be stuck slogging through *two* books."

All true, possibly. But if you just don't get it, maybe it's because the *author* just doesn't know how to *explain* it. *Maybe it's not your fault!* Too many students have sweated, moaned, dropped classes, even changed majors because they thought they were dumb, when it's possible it's the darned textbook that's dense, not you. So instead of continuing to slog though the mire, find an expert who can actually write — they're out there — and learn what you need to. After finally understanding the subject by reading this other text, you'll find much of the original textbook much easier to use...presuming you need it at all.

CHAPTER 2

Reading with Purpose

VEN IF YOU consider yourself "not much of a reader," you read *something* each and every day: a magazine article, instructions for hooking up the DVD player, telephone messages tacked on the refrigerator, notes from your latest heartthrob.

Regardless of *what* you are reading, you have a purpose that dictates *how* you are going to read it—and you read different items in different ways. You wouldn't read the DVD player instructions as you would a novel, any more than you'd read the magazine article in the same way as a grocery list. Without a purpose, you'd find yourself reading aimlessly and very inefficiently.

Unfortunately, many of the students I've talked to have not yet realized the importance of having a purpose for reading. Their lack of reading purpose can be summed up by the proverb, "If you aim at nothing, you will hit the bull's-eye every time."

Before you can understand what you're reading—and _remember_ it—you must know _why_ you're reading it in the first place.

Defining your purpose for reading

What is your purpose for reading? If the best answer you can come up with is, "Because my teacher said so," we need to come up with some better reasons. Reading a chapter just so you can say, "I finished my assignment," is relatively futile. You may as well put the book under a pillow and hope to absorb it by osmosis.

Unless you identify some purpose to read, you will find yourself flipping the pages of your textbooks while seldom retaining anything more than the chapter titles.

According to reading experts, there are six fundamental purposes for reading:

1. To grasp a certain message.
2. To find important details.
3. To answer a specific question.
4. To evaluate what you are reading.
5. To apply what you are reading.
6. To be entertained.

Because reading with purpose is the first step toward improved comprehension, let me suggest some simple techniques you can use to identify a purpose for _your_ textbook reading.

Find the clues in every book

There is a group of special sections found in nearly all textbooks and technical materials (in fact, in almost all books except novels) that contain a wealth of information and can help you glean more from your reading. Becoming familiar with this data will enrich your reading experience and often make it easier. Here's what to look for:

The first page after the title page is usually the *table of contents* — a chapter-by-chapter list of the book's contents. Some are surprisingly detailed, listing every major point or topic covered in each chapter.

The first prose section (after the title page, table of contents, and, perhaps, *acknowledgments page*, in which the author thanks other authors, his editor, researcher, friends, relatives, teachers, and so forth, most of which you can ignore), is the *preface*, usually a description of what information you will find in the book. Authors may also use the preface to point out unique aspects of their books.

The *introduction* may be in place of or in addition to the preface and may be written by the author or some "name" the author has recruited to lend additional prestige to his or her work. Most introductions are an even more detailed overview of the book — chapter-by-chapter summaries are often included to give the reader a feel for the material to be covered.

Footnotes may be found throughout the text (a slightly elevated number following a sentence, quotation, or paragraph, for example, "jim-dandy"[24]) and either explained at the bottom of the page on which they appear or in a special section at the back of the text. Footnotes may be used to cite sources of direct quotes or ideas and/or to further explain a point, add information, and so forth, outside of the text. You may make it a habit to ferret out sources cited for further reading.

If a text tends to use an alarmingly high number of terms with which you may not be familiar, the considerate author will include a *glossary* — essentially an abridged dictionary that defines all such terms.

The *bibliography*, usually at the end of the book, may include the source material the author used to research the textbook, a list of "recommended reading," or both. It is usually organized alphabetically by subject, making it easy for you to go to your library and find more information on a specific topic.

Appendices containing supplementary data or examples relating to subject matter covered in the text may also appear in the back of the book.

The last thing in a book is usually the *index*, an alphabetical listing that references, by page number, every mention of a particular name, subject, and topic in the text.

Making it a habit to utilize all of these tools in your textbook can only make your studying easier.

Look for the clues in each chapter

Every textbook offers some clues that will help you define a purpose for reading. Begin with a very quick overview of the assignment, looking for questions that you'd like answered. Consider the following elements of your reading assignment *before* you begin your reading.

Much like the headlines of a newspaper clue you into what the story is about, these elements will give insight into what the section or chapter is trying to communicate:

Chapter heads and subheads

Chapter titles and bold-faced subheads announce the detail about the main topic. And, in some textbooks, paragraph headings or bold-face "lead-ins" announce that the author is about to provide finer details.

So start each reading assignment by going through the chapter, beginning to end, *reading only the bold-faced heads and subheads.*

For example, suppose you encountered the heading, "The Fall of Communism," in your history textbook. You might use it to formulate the following questions:

1. *What* caused the fall of Communism?
2. *Who* caused it?
3. *When* did it fall?
4. *Why* did it fall?
5. *Where* did the fall occur?

As you read the chapter, you'll find yourself seeking answers to these questions. You now have a purpose!

Often you may find headings that contain words or terms you don't recognize. Seeking to define these terms or explain a concept should then become your purpose.

This process of headline reading takes only a few minutes, but it lays the groundwork for a more intelligent and efficient reading of the chapter. You'll have some idea where the author is headed, which will help you identify the most important details and clarify where you should be concentrating your studying.

End-of-chapter summaries

If you read a mystery from start to finish, the way the author hopes you will, you're likely to get thrown off the scent by "red herrings" and other common detective novel devices. However, if you read the last page first, knowing the outcome will help you detect how the author constructed the novel and built an open-and-shut case for his or her master sleuth. You'd perceive a wealth of details about the eventually unmasked murderer that might have gone *un*-noticed had he been just another of the leading suspects.

Similarly, knowing what the author is driving at in a *textbook* will help you look for the important building blocks for his conclusions while you're reading.

It may not be fun to read a mystery novel this way, but when it comes to textbook reading, it will help you define your purpose for reading. And further, it will transform you into a much more *active* reader, making it less likely you'll doze off while being beaten senseless by the usual ponderous prose.

Pictures, graphs, and charts

Most textbooks, particularly those in the sciences, will have charts, graphs, numerical tables, maps, and other illustrations. All too many students see these as fillers — padding to glance at quickly, and, just as quickly, forget.

If you're giving these charts and graphs short shrift, you're really shortchanging _yourself._ Be sure to observe how they supplement the text, understand what points they emphasize, and make note of these.

Highlighted terms, vocabulary, and other facts

In some textbooks, you'll discover that key terms and information are highlighted within the body text. (I don't mean highlighted by a previous student — treat such yellow-markered passages with caution!) To find the definitions of these terms, or to find the application of facts, may then be your purpose for reading.

Questions

Some textbook publishers use a format in which key points are emphasized by questions, either within the body of text or at the end of the chapter. If you read these questions _before_ reading the chapter, you'll have a better idea of what material you need to pay closer attention to.

Prereading your assignment

If you begin your reading assignment by seeking out these heads, subheads, and other purpose-finding elements of the chapter, you'll have completed your prereading step.

What is prereading? It is simply beginning your assigned reading by reviewing these clues and defining your purpose (or purposes) for reading.

I advise that you *always* preread every assignment! Why? Have you ever spent the better part of an evening plowing through an assignment only to finish with little or no understanding of what you just read? If the answer is yes, then you probably failed to preread it.

Reading faster without speed reading

While the heads, subheads, first sentences, and other author-provided hints we've talked about will help you get a quick read on what a chapter's about, some of the *words* in that chapter will help you concentrate on the important points and ignore the unimportant. Knowing when to speed up, slow down, ignore, or really concentrate will help you read both faster *and* more effectively.

When you see words and phrases such as "likewise," "in addition," "moreover," "furthermore," and the like, you should know nothing new is being introduced. If you already know what's going on, speed up or skip what's coming entirely.

On the other hand, when you see "on the other hand," "nevertheless," "however," "rather," "but," and their ilk, slow down—you're getting information that adds a new perspective or contradicts what you've just read.

Lastly, watch out for payoff words and phrases such as, "to summarize," "in conclusion," "therefore," "consequently," "thus"—especially if you only have time to "hit the high points" of a chapter or you're reviewing for a test. Here's where the real meat is, where everything that went before is happily tied up in a nice bow and ribbon, a present that enables you to avoid having to unwrap the entire chapter.

Purpose defines reading method

Typically, your purpose for reading dictates how you read. There are basically three types of reading we all do:

1. **Quick reference reading** focuses on seeking specific information that addresses a particular question or concern we might have.
2. **Critical reading** involves discerning ideas and concepts that require a thorough analysis.
3. **Aesthetic, or pleasure reading,** is what we do for sheer entertainment or to appreciate an author's style and ability.

As you define your purpose for reading, you will determine which method of reading is necessary to accomplish this purpose. In the following table are some examples of types of reading, why you might read them, and the method you should use:

Type	Purpose	Method
Newspaper advertisement	To locate best price for car	Quick reference
Magazine	To stay aware of current events	Quick reference
Self-help book	To learn to get along better with your family	Critical
Biology text	To prepare for an exam	Critical
New issue of _Rolling Stone_	To take your mind off biology!	Pleasure

If you're a good reader or desire to be one: You will always fit your reading *method* to your reading *purpose;* you have trained or are training yourself in a variety of reading skills; you have no problem switching your method to accommodate your purpose; and you are unsatisfied reading only one type of material.

A poor reader, on the other hand, reads everything the same way—doggedly plowing through the biology assignment, the newspaper, and the Stephen King novel...word by painful word. Reading with purpose is both foreign and foreboding to such a person, which makes it difficult for him or her to adapt a method of reading.

Become an active reader

Reading with purpose is as vital to your comprehension and retention as oxygen is to life. It is the cornerstone of *active* reading, reading that involves thinking—that process of engaging your mind and emotions in what the author is trying to communicate. Too many readers seek to absorb information passively as their eyes move across the page. The active reader *involves* him- or herself in receiving a message—a fact, an idea, an opinion—that is readily retained because he or she had a *purpose*.

✎✎✎

Following is a passage adapted from *101 Ways to Make Every Second Count* by Robert W. Bly (Career Press, 1999). *Preread* the passage in order to determine a *purpose* for reading. Be sure to use the notes page following the passage to jot down questions that may have been raised through your preread, as well as your purpose:

Learn to handle pressure and juggle projects

Are you too busy? If you've been in the corporate world for a spell, you know how difficult it can be to cope with an overload of work. Here are some suggestions for doing so.

Learn to say no. It's scary to turn down work or say no to a manager above you. But when you're truly too busy, it's sometimes the best thing to do. After all, if you take on more than you can handle and miss a deadline or do shoddy work in order to make the deadline, that will do far more harm to your relationship and reputation than saying no.

I rarely say no to current clients, unless the deadline is so tight that I cannot possibly make it. If that's the case, I ask if there's any reason why the deadline can't be a few days longer, and I usually get it. (Many deadlines are artificial and have no logic behind them.) If they cannot be flexible, I politely explain that the deadline is too short, thank them for the offer of the job, apologize for not being able to take it on, and suggest they give it to one of their other resources (freelancers, in-house staff, ad agency, production studio).

However, I frequently say no to new prospects who call me during a busy period. When they start to describe their project or ask about my service, I stop them and say, "I'd be delighted to talk with you about this project. But I don't want to waste your time, so I must tell you now that I am booked through the end of September [or whenever]. If the project is not a rush or if you can delay it until then, I'd be happy to work with you. If not, I'll have to pass."

Amazingly, the usual reaction is not anger or hostility (although a few callers get mad); instead, most are impressed, even amazed. ("You mean you are booked through September? Boy, you must be good!" one caller said today.) In fact, turning down work because you are booked frequently creates the immediate impression that you are in demand and thus tops in your field, creating an even stronger desire to work with you. Many people you turn down will call you back at the time you specify and ask, almost reverently, always respectfully, "You said call back in September. I have a project. Can you work with me now?" Try it. It works!

Set the parameters. An alternative to turning down work cold is to set the schedule and deadline according to your convenience, not theirs. "Well, I am booked fairly solidly," you tell the prospect. "I can squeeze you in; however, it will take seven weeks [or whatever] instead of the usual three to complete your project, because of my schedule. If you can wait this long, I'll be happy to help you. If not, I will have to pass on the assignment."

Again, many prospects will turn to someone who can accommodate their original deadline. However, many others will say "yes" to your request and hire you on your terms.

Get up an hour earlier. I find that mornings are my most productive time. I work best from 7 a.m., when I usually start, to 1 or 2 p.m.; after that, I slow down. If I am extremely busy, I try to start at 6 a.m. instead of 7 a.m. and find that I get an amazing amount of work done during that first extra hour. Also, it makes me less panicky for the rest of the day because I have accomplished so much so early.

Work an hour later or work one or two hours in the evenings after dinner. If you usually knock off at 5 p.m., go to 6 p.m. Or, if you generally watch television from 8 p.m. to 10 p.m., work an extra hour and a half from 10 p.m. to 11:30 p.m. I prefer the extra morning hour for client projects; evening time is reserved for my own self-sponsored projects, such as books, articles, or self-publishing.

Put in half a day Saturday morning or Saturday afternoon. If you have to work weekends, Saturday morning — say, from 8 a.m. to noon — is the best time. You get that early morning energy and get the work out of the way so you can relax and enjoy the rest of the weekend. If you are not a morning person, try Saturday afternoon. If you put the work off until Sunday, you'll probably just spend all Saturday worrying about it or feeling guilty about it, so don't. Get it done first thing and then forget about it.

Hire a temp. If you are under a crunch consider getting temporary help for such tasks as proofreading, editing, research, typing, data entry, trips to the post office, and library research. Spend the money to get rid of unnecessary administrative burdens and free yourself to concentrate on the important tasks in front of you.

Break complex tasks into smaller, bite-size segments. Rush jobs are intimidating. If you have two weeks to work a major brochure, but put it off until the last three or four days, the task looms large and panic can set in.

The solution is to break the project into subprojects, assign a certain amount of the task to each day remaining, and then write this down on a sheet of paper and post it on the wall or bulletin board in front of your desk.

Ask for more time. When you are just starting out, you naturally want to please co-workers and thus you agree to any deadline they suggest. In fact, you encourage tight deadlines because you believe that doing the work fast is a sign of doing your job right.

As you get older and more experienced, you learn two important truths. First, that many deadlines are artificial and can be comfortably extended with no negative effect on the client's needs whatsoever. And second, that it's more important to take the time to do the job right then to try and impress a naive client or supervisor by doing it fast. What matters, for example, is not that the software was coded fast but that it works, meets user requirements, is reliable, and doesn't have bugs. So if you need extra time, ask for it. This is real service to the client. Doing rush jobs is not.

Get a fax machine. Before the advent of the fax machine, if I had a project due Wednesday, I pretty much had to be done with it on Tuesday at 3 p.m. so it could be printed and ready for Federal Express pick-up by 5 p.m. Now with a fax machine, the job due Wednesday can be finished Wednesday at 4 p.m. and on the client's desk at 4:15 p.m. — giving me an extra day on every project.

Most corporate workers I know have fax machines. Some entrepreneurs don't. If your small business doesn't have one, get one. Don't waste time and money faxing documents at the local stationery store. Don't waste your time or other peoples' by making your fax compete with your modem and phone for use of one line; get separate lines for each. (Having the same number for phone and fax also is a sign to some people that you are not running a "real" business.)

Stay seated. Georges Simenon, author of the popular *Inspector Maigret* series of mystery novels, wrote more than 500 books. How did he do it? Simenon said that he limited his writing vocabulary to 2,000 words so he would not have to use a dictionary (there are more than 800,000 words in the English language, with 60,000 new words added since 1966). This allowed him to work continuously, without having to stop, open, and search a dictionary for a word. The key to his success then, at least in part, was working without interruption—he kept going, and didn't let anything stop him while he was hot.

You've heard the term "seat of the pants" used to describe a method of working. Although it originally referred to a person who made decisions by instinct without a lot of planning or formal study, for office workers the definition is different: You apply the bottom of your pants (your rear end) to the seat (your chair), and stay there until the work gets done.

This means getting into your chair—and staying there. No using the VCR monitor in your office to watch TV. No quick trips to the cafeteria for a snack. No gossiping around the water cooler. This sounds trivial, but is in fact an important point. To get a lot of work done, workers must stay at their workstations. For office workers, the workstation is your desk and chair. Distractions are death to peak personal productivity. It's bad enough that many distractions—drop-in visitors, emergencies, telemarketing calls—already present themselves during a normal workday. Do not seek them out deliberately.

Your notes

What clues can you find that help you define a purpose for reading this passage?

_____

_____

_____

_____

_____

What purpose or purposes did you determine for reading this passage?

_____

_____

_____

_____

_____

What method, based on your purpose, would you use to read this passage?

_____

_____

_____

_____

_____

_____

_____

_____

_____

CHAPTER 3

Finding the Main Idea

I N ALL GOOD writing, there is a controlling thesis or message that connects all of the specific details and facts. This concept or idea is usually expressed as a generalization that summarizes the entire text.

Good comprehension results when you are able to grasp this main message, even if you sometimes forget some of the details. When you understand the intent, you have a context in which to evaluate the reasoning, the attitude, and whether the evidence cited really is supportive of the conclusions drawn.

An obsession for facts can obscure the "big picture," giving you an understanding of the trees but no concept of the forest. How many of you have spent hours studying for an important exam, collecting dates, names, terms, and formulas, but failed to ferret out the main idea, the underlying concept that is composed of these facts?

In longer, more involved readings, many messages are combined to form a chain of thought, which, in turn, may or may not be communicating one thesis or idea.

Your ability to capture this chain of thought determines your level of comprehension — and what you retain.

Dissecting your reading assignment

To succeed in identifying the main idea in any reading assignment, you must learn to use these helpful tools:

1. The topic sentence of a paragraph.
2. Summary sentences.
3. Supporting sentences.
4. Transitional statements.

As you learn to dissect your reading assignment paragraph by paragraph, identifying its many parts and their functions, you'll grasp the main idea much more quickly — and remember it much longer.

Recognizing a topic sentence

Every paragraph has a _topic sentence_ — the sentence that summarizes what the paragraph is about. Even if a paragraph does not have such a clearly stated sentence, it can be implied or inferred from what is written.

Generally, the topic sentence is the first or last sentence of a paragraph — the one statement that announces, "Here's what this paragraph is all about!"

When the topic sentence is obscured or hidden, you may need to utilize two simple exercises to uncover it:

1. Pretend you're a headline writer for your local newspaper — write a headline for the paragraph you just read.
2. Write a five-word summary describing what the paragraph is about.

Exercise: Identifying a topic sentence

Write a headline or five-word summary for each of the following paragraphs:

Working and debt collection don't mix. Whatever your reasons for not paying your debts, you have the right to keep your private financial affairs from becoming common office knowledge. Harassment at work or any place is illegal. However, it's not illegal for a debt collector to call you at work — unless you tell the collector it's inconvenient for you. Any collector who calls to discuss payments of your debt after you've said not to is breaking the law.

Today your entire job search can be conducted online. With a computer and modem, you can dial up a database containing tens of thousands of detailed, current job listings in your industry or occupation or conduct research on prospective employers. You can also multiply your own visibility by placing your resume online where it can be viewed by an increasing number of employers, agencies, and recruiters with jobs to fill.

Day trading, however, can provide you with an opportunity to make money in the short term without waiting years to see the results. While your long-term portfolio is dependent on the belief that with time the market tends to go up, day trading allows you to take advantage of the current, short-term market environment. You must never forget that although our stock market has done extremely well during the last 60 years, there is no guarantee the good times will continue.

✎✎✎

As you can see from these three paragraphs, the topic sentence is not always clearly stated. This is especially true in a number of the convoluted textbooks all of us have read. When trying to discern the main idea of such writing, you may need a more in-depth analysis.

You can begin your analysis by turning, once again, to our helpful questions. Is the passage written to address one of the following questions?

1. **Who?** The paragraph focuses on a particular person or group of people. The topic sentence tells you _who_ this is.

2. **When?** The paragraph is primarily concerned with _time_. The topic sentence may even begin with the word "when."

3. **Where?** The paragraph is oriented around a particular place or location. The topic sentence states _where_ you are reading about.

4. **Why?** A paragraph that states reasons for some belief or happening usually addresses this question. The topic sentence answers _why_ something is true or _why_ an event happened.

5. **How?** A paragraph that identifies the way something works or the means by which something is done. The topic sentence explains the _how_ of what is described.

You will notice that I did not include the question "What?" in this list. This is not an oversight. "What?" addresses such a broad range of possibilities that asking this question will not necessarily lead you to the topic sentence.

The best test to determine whether you have identified the topic sentence is to rephrase it as a question. If the paragraph answers the question that you've framed, you've found the topic sentence.

Summary, support, or transitional?

Another technique that will lead you to the topic sentence is to identify what purpose *other* sentences in the paragraph serve — kind of a process of elimination.

Generally, sentences can be characterized as *summary, support,* or *transitional.*

Summary sentences state a general idea or concept. As a rule, a topic sentence is a summary sentence — a concise yet inclusive statement that expresses the general intent of the paragraph. (By definition, the topic sentence is never a support sentence.)

Support sentences provide the specific details and facts that give credibility to the author's points of view. They give examples, explain arguments, offer evidence, or attempt to prove something as true or false. They are not meant to state generally what the author wants to communicate — they are intended to be specific, not conceptual, in nature.

Transitional sentences help the author move from one point to another. They may be viewed as bridges connecting the paragraphs in a text, suggesting the relationship between what you just finished reading and what you are about to read. Good readers are attuned to the signals such sentences provide — they are buzzers that scream, "This is what you are going to find out next!"

Transitional sentences may also alert you to what you should have just learned. Unlike support sentences, transitional sentences provide invaluable and direct clues to identifying the topic sentence.

Some examples of transitional signals

Any sentence that continues a progression of thought or succession of concepts is a transitional sentence. Such a sentence may begin with a word such as "first," "next," "finally," or "then" and indicate the before/after connection between changes, improvements, or alterations.

Transitional sentences that begin in this way should raise these questions in your mind:

1. Do I know what the previous examples were?
2. What additional example am I about to learn?
3. What was the situation prior to the change?

Other transition statements suggest a change in argument or thought or an exception to a rule. These will generally be introduced by words such as "but," "although," "though," "rather," "however," or similar conjunctions that suggest an opposing thought.

Such words ought to raise these questions:

1. What is the gist of the argument I just read?
2. What will the argument I am about to read state?
3. To what rule is the author offering an exception?

In your effort to improve your reading, developing the ability to recognize the contrast between general, inclusive words and statements (summary sentences) and specific, detail-oriented sentences (transitional or support sentences) is paramount.

Taking notes

The final step toward grasping and retaining the main idea of any paragraph is taking notes. There are several traditional methods students employ — outlining, highlighting, mapping, and drawing concept trees.

An exhaustive review of all these methods is not within the scope of this particular book, but for a complete discussion of note-taking techniques, be sure to read *Take Notes*, another of the books in my *How to Study Program.*

Whichever method you employ to retain the main idea, focus on the topic sentences, not on the specific details.

If you are a highlighter — you enjoy coloring textbooks with fluorescent markers — you will want to assign one color that you will always use to highlight topic sentences. Avoid what too many students do — highlighting virtually every paragraph. This practice will just extend your review time considerably — you'll find yourself rereading instead of reviewing.

If you utilize outlining or mapping (diagramming what you read rather than spending time worrying about Roman numerals and whether to use lower case letters or upper case letters on certain lines) you will find that your time will best be spent writing five-word summaries of the topic sentences.

If you find yourself getting bogged down in details and specifics, you are wasting valuable time. Again, writers are using these details to communicate their concepts — they are not necessarily to be remembered.

☙☙☙

Read the following passage from *International Business Etiquette: Latin America* by Ann Marie Sabath (Career Press, 2000), seeking out the topic sentences. Then summarize the main idea or ideas in five-word phrases.

Business Entertaining in Argentina

Argentines believe that building and developing trust with individuals is paramount for establishing business relationships. One way that these relationships are developed is by spending time together during meals. Business dinners are the norm, because many Argentines return to their homes for lunch.

When you are invited to dinner, prepare to meet around 10 p.m. and to be together for at least two hours. Conversation will focus most likely on social topics rather than the business at hand. Wait to discuss business only if it is brought up by your host; otherwise, you may risk offending your Argentine contact.

Beef is a very common meat in Argentina. However, you should expect to be served some foods that may be slightly different than the cuisine to which you are accustomed — for example, cow brains, intestines, kidneys, and so on. Even if you've never wanted to try these foods before, it is considered proper to at least taste them rather than to risk offending your Argentine host by refusing them. Besides, you can always make up for it with special culinary treats, including the delicious _helado_, which is Argentinian ice cream.

Table manners: As in other Latin American countries, the continental style of using utensils is adopted in Argentina — that is, keep your fork in your left hand with the tines down and your knife in your right hand with the serrated edge facing the plate. When not using your utensils, be sure to keep your hands on the table at all times, as hands below the table is considered poor manners. To signal that you have finished eating, lay your knife and fork parallel on the plate, with the handles to the right.

If you are invited to join your Argentine contact between 4 p.m. and 6 p.m., then you will probably be enjoying "tea." This will most likely be comprised of coffee (which may taste like espresso to North Americans) and dessert foods.

Because Argentines are a very proud people, they may insist on paying the bill whether or not they have initiated the meal invitation. When you are hosting the meal, in order to prevent a "tug of war," you should make arrangements with the wait staff to pay for the meal beforehand or by excusing yourself from the table at an appropriate moment. If you are not able to do this, then you may have to insist repeatedly on paying the bill.

If you are a woman, note that *machismo* is very prevalent in Argentina. Therefore, an Argentine man would be very embarrassed if a women paid for the meal or even offered to pay for the meal. As a female host, if you wish to pay the bill, it is best to arrange for a male associate or family member to take care of it on your behalf.

Finally, as in many countries, do not wait for the server to bring the bill to the table; it will be presented only after you request it.

✎✎✎

Let's try again with this brief excerpt from, "Europe's Back Doors" by George Stoltz, which appeared in the January 2000 edition of *The Atlantic Monthly*:

In 1995 several nations in the European Union began to enact the Schengen Accords, by which internal EU borders were weakened and external borders were strengthened, and entry into Spain became a virtual guarantee of unimpeded passage to Germany, France, or nearly any other EU country—a powerful temptation for a potential immigrant. And Spain has not been spared the shrinking labor pools and restructuring economies that have affected nearly all industrialized nations. Like its Northern European neighbors, Spain needs guest workers to harvest its crops, build its buildings, clean its houses, and labor in its factories.

Significant numbers of illegal immigrants from sub-Saharan Africa began appearing in Ceuta and Melilla in the mid-1990s, almost as soon as the accords started to go into effect, and nearly 12,000 have made their way there so far. At least 6,000 entered Ceuta illegally last year. Despite Spain's attempts at vigilance and prevention, perhaps twenty to twenty-five Africans reach Ceuta daily, and some 10,000 are said to be biding their time in nearby Moroccan cities such as Tangier and Tetouan, waiting their turn for experienced local smugglers to show them how, when, and where to cross the border.

These figures are not large in comparison with immigration figures for other EU nations, such as Germany and France, and tiny in comparison with the number of legal and illegal immigrants who enter the United States each year. But they are certain to grow. The Spanish Foreign Ministry estimates that Europe will see up to 25 million legal and illegal immigrants over the next 10 years, with the bulk coming from Africa; if such predictions prove correct, the impact on Spain will be great.

"The figures are small, but the phenomenon itself is new," says Hector Maravall, the director of Spain's National immigration and Social Services Institute. "Today there are about ten thousand immigrants out of all Africa, including Morocco, into Spain each year. If you compare that with the immigration pressure on Germany or even Italy, it's nothing. But four or five years ago there were five hundred annually to Spain. You have to ask, What is going to be happening five years from now?"

✎✎✎

The author is throwing around a lot of statistics to impress upon his readers that the growing number of illegal African immigrants coming through Spain to get to other European countries is alarming. Should we remember the statistics about how many immigrants entered Cueta, how many are waiting in Morocco to cross the border, or how many are predicted to enter over the next 10 years? Should these statistics appear in our notes?

If we read linearly, starting at the beginning and plodding along to the last word, we probably would be tempted to write down these numbers and what they mean in our notes. But, if we were to look ahead in the article, we'd find that the author is actually using Ceuta and Melilla merely to illustrate the larger problem of illegal immigration. Therefore, the statistics are not especially important, but the enormity of the problem to which they give credence *is*.

I didn't always keep my summaries to five words, but I distilled the main ideas to the fewest words I could.

Nor did I always write one summary statement per paragraph—just what was needed to capture the main idea or ideas from each paragraph.

CHAPTER 4

Gathering the Facts

> Now, what I want is Facts. Teach these boys and girls nothing but Facts. Facts alone are wanted in life. Plant nothing else, and root out everything else. You can only form the minds of reasoning animals upon Facts: Nothing else will ever be of any service to them. This is the principle on which I bring up my own children, and this is the principle on which I bring up these children. Stick to Facts, sir!

— Charles Dickens, *Hard Times*

EEKING OUT THE facts, as Dickens' character would have us do, is also an effective way to confront your classroom reading assignments.

While such an approach is not the whole formula for scholastic success, you'll find that the vast majority of your assigned reading requires a thorough recall of the facts.

In the previous chapter, we discussed the "forest" — the main idea. In this chapter, we will concentrate on "the trees" — how to read to gather facts, the specific details that support and develop the author's main point.

Facts: Building blocks for ideas

Facts are the building blocks that give credibility to concepts and ideas. Your ability to gather and assimilate these facts will dramatically enhance your success at remembering what the author wanted to communicate.

If, however, you spend so much time studying the trees that you lose sight of the forest, your reading effectiveness will be limited. You must learn to differentiate between facts that are salient to your understanding and those best left for the next *Trivial Pursuit* update.

If you are trying to identify your purpose for reading this chapter, it's three-fold:

1. To develop the skill of scanning a text for facts as quickly as possible.
2. To distinguish between an important detail and a trivial one.
3. To learn how to *skim* text—reading and absorbing its essence, even when you're not looking for anything in particular.

Deciphering the message

The author of any kind of writing should have something to say, a message to communicate.

Unfortunately, such messages are often lost in the glut of verbiage many authors use to "dress up" their basic point. It's your job to rake through the mess and get to the heart of the text.

You need to approach each reading assignment with the mindset of Sherlock Holmes: There is a mystery to be solved, and you are the master detective. The goal is to figure out what the text is trying to communicate—regardless of how deeply it is buried in the quagmire of convoluted language.

What is the message?

The first step in any good investigation is to collect all of the clues. What are the facts? By spending a few minutes of your time discerning these concrete facts, you will be far better equipped to digest what it is the author is trying to communicate.

But how do you extract the facts when they appear to be hidden in an impenetrable forest of words? You may need a little help—from "who-what-when-where-why-and-how." It seems that the facts readily sally forth when these six trusty questions are called upon the scene.

✎✎✎

Exercise: Read the following excerpt, keeping these six words in mind. After you have finished reading it, answer the questions that follow. Be careful—you may have to slow way down!

Odds are you'll never meet any of the estimated 247 human beings who were born in the past minute. In a population of 6 billion, 247 is a demographic hiccup. In the minute before last, however, there were another 247. In the minutes to come there will be another, then another, then another. By next year at this time, all those minutes will have produced 130 million newcomers to the great human mosh pit. Even after subtracting the deaths each year, the world population is still the equivalent of adding one new Germany.

The last time humanity celebrated a new century there were 1.6 billion people here for the party—or a quarter as many as this time. In 1900 the average life expectancy was, in some places, as low as 23 years; now it's 65, meaning the extra billions are staying around longer and demanding more from the planet.

But things may not be as bleak as they seem. In country after country, birthrates are easing, and the population growth rate is falling.

Cheering as the population reports are becoming today, for much of the past 50 years, demographers were bearers of mostly bad tidings. It was not until the century was nearly two-thirds over that scientists and governments finally bestirred themselves to do something about it. The first great brake on population growth came in the 1960s, with the development of the birth-control pill. In 1969 the United Nations created the U.N. Population Fund, a global organization dedicated to bringing family-planning techniques to women who would not otherwise have them.

Such efforts have paid off in a big way. According to U.N. head counters, the average number of children produced per couple in the developing world—a figure that reached 4.9 earlier this century—has plunged to just 2.7.

But bringing down birthrates loses some of its effectiveness as mortality rates also fall. When people live longer, populations grow not just bigger but also older and frailer.

For now the answer may be to tough things out for a while, waiting for the billions of people born during the great population boom to live out their long lives, while at the same time continuing to reduce birthrates further so that things don't get thrown out of kilter again.

According to three scenarios published by the U.N., the global population in the year 2050 will be somewhere between 7.3 billion and 10.7 billion, depending on how fast the fertility rate falls. The difference between the high scenario and the low scenario? Just one child per couple.

✎✎✎

1. At the world's current growth rate, each year the number of people born is akin to the number of people in _____*C*_____.
  a. China
  b. the United States
  c. Germany
  d. France

2. The average number of children each couple have in the developing world is now ___.
   a. 1.6
   b. 2.7
   c. 4.9
   d. 6.3

3. World population is expected to be between 7.3 and 10.7 billion in the year ___.
   a. 2010
   b. 2025
   c. 2050
   d. 2100

4. The first major brake on population growth is credited to ___.
   a. Germany
   b. the fall of world mortality rates
   c. the U.N. Population Fund
   d. the birth-control pill

5. What would be the best title for this passage?
   a. Overpopulation: How We Got Here and Where to Go
   b. What to Do with an Overpopulated Planet
   c. Family-Planning for the New Millennium
   d. The Importance of Birthrates

In the preceding exercise, you should have quickly read through the text and been able to answer all five questions. If it took you more than three minutes to do so, you spent too much time. You were reading *only* to answer our six questions — "who?", "what?", "when?", "where?", "why?", and "how?" Your purpose was to identify the facts, nothing more.

Scanning, skimming, reading, remembering

Most everyone I know confuses *skim* and *scan*. Let me set the record straight. *Skim is to read quickly and superficially. Scan is to read carefully but for a specific item.* So when you *skim* a reading selection, you are reading it in its entirety, though you're only hitting the "highlights."

When you *scan* a selection, you are reading it in detail but only until you find what you're looking for. Scanning is the technique we all employ when using the phone book—unless, of course, you're in the habit of reading every name in the book to find the one you're looking for. When you scan, your eyes do not look at every word, read every sentence, or think about every paragraph. Instead, they rapidly move across the page to find just what you are looking for and then read that carefully.

Scanning is the *fastest* reading rate of all—although you are reading in detail, you are *not* seeking to comprehend or remember anything that you see until you find the bit of information you're looking for.

When I was in college, I would begin any assignment by reading the first sentence of every paragraph and trying to answer the questions at the chapter's end. If this did not give me a pretty good idea of the content and important details of that chapter, then—and only then—would I read it more thoroughly.

I'm sure this method of skimming for the facts saved me countless hours of time (and boredom).

Ask first, then look

When skimming for detail, you will often have a particular question, date, or fact to find. You should approach the text much like the dictionary—knowing the word, you just scan the pages to find its definition. If you must answer a specific question or read about a historic figure, you simply find a source — book, magazine, encyclopedia, or Web site — and quickly scan the text for the answer or person.

You probably are assigned a lot of reading that can be accomplished by skimming for facts. By establishing the questions you want answered *before* you begin to read, you can quickly browse through the material, extracting only the information you need.

Let's say you're reading a science book with the goal of identifying the function of the cell's nucleus. You can breeze through the section that gives the parts of the cell. You can skim the description of what cells do. You already know what you're looking for. And there it is in the section that talks about what each cell part does. Now you can start to *read*.

By identifying the questions you wanted to answer (*a.k.a.* your purpose) in advance, you would be able to skim the chapter and answer your questions in a lot less time than it would have taken to painstakingly read every word.

As a general rule, if you are reading textbook material word for word, you probably are wasting quite a bit of your study time. Good readers are able to discern what they should read in this manner and what they can afford to skim. When trying to simply gather detail and facts, skimming a text is a simple and very important shortcut.

Alternatively, our ability to skim a chapter — even something you need to read more critically — will enable you to develop a general sense of what the chapter is about and how thoroughly it needs to be read.

✎✎✎

Exercise: Answer the following questions by skimming the paragraph that follows.

    1. How many miles of coastline does Brazil have?

2. Which two South American countries do not border Brazil?
3. Which river is Brazil home to?

The largest country in South America is also the fifth-largest country in the world. The Republic of Brazil is a vast land covering more than 3.3 million square miles, nearly half of the continent, with 4,600 miles of coastline looking out into the Atlantic Ocean. Brazil borders every country in South America except for Chile and Ecuador. This huge nation is home to a variety of climates and natural attractions, including immense rainforests and the world's largest river, the Amazon.

If this were part of your assigned reading, you would be finished when you had answered the questions. "But I didn't read it," you protest. Can you write a one-sentence summary of the paragraph? If you *can*, and you answered the questions correctly, then you know all you need to.

Skimming, or prereading, is a valuable step even if you aren't seeking specific facts. When skimming for a general overview, there's a very simple procedure to follow:

1. If there is a title or heading, *rephrase it as a question.* This will be your purpose for reading.
2. Examine all the *subheadings, illustrations,* and *graphics,* as these will help you identify the significant matter within the text.
3. Read thoroughly the *introductory paragraphs,* the summary, and any questions at the chapter's end.
4. Read the *first sentence* of every paragraph. As we found in Chapter 3, this is generally where the main idea of a text is found.

5. *Evaluate* what you have gained from this process: Can you answer the questions at the end of the chapter? Could you intelligently participate in a class discussion of the material?
6. *Write* a brief summary that encapsulates what you have learned from your skimming.
7. Based on this evaluation, *decide* whether a more thorough reading is required.

✎✎✎

Exercise: Let's see how well you can skim for an overview, rather than for specific facts. Read the following two passages, then follow the seven steps outlined previously for each.

The Brain

The brain is subdivided into four major areas. From the top down, you'll find: 1) the *cerebral cortex,* which I refer to as the cortex; 2) the *midbrain,* which contains a lot of the switching areas where nerves that pass up from below go to and from the cortex; 3) the *brainstem,* where much of the basic nervous system controls sit (coma occurs when this malfunctions, and death occurs when it is severed); and 4) the *cerebellum,* which sits behind the upper part of the brainstem and has traditionally been thought to regulate coordination of complex movements.

The cerebral cortex is the most newly evolved region of the brain and it is the part that separates humans from all the other mammals, especially the area in the front, appropriately named the *frontal cortex.* This area acts as a bridge between the sensory and motor circuits of the rest of the cortex and the older, deeper structures of the limbic system, which regulate drive and emotion. The frontal cortex is probably where much of our complex and abstract thoughts occur. It is probably where we put today in context with yesterday and tomorrow. When the frontal lobe is damaged, we become either more reactive and hypersexual like wild animals (without the step of logic in between to stop us) or very docile and unconcerned.

Behind the frontal cortex are the sensory and motor regions of the cortex, each divided up to correspond with specific areas on the opposite side of the body. Along the side are two protruding horns of cortex called the *temporal lobes*. Here, much of the processing of sound and verbal information occurs. Inside sits a deeper part of the limbic system called the *hippocampus*. The hippocampus acts like a way-station that coordinates the placement of information as it moves from sensory input to other areas of the brain.

In the back is the *occipital cortex*, where much of the processing of visual information occurs. The remaining areas along the side above the temporal horns form the *parietal cortex*. These areas are thought to be where a lot of cross-connection between the different sensory structures occurs. When the right side of the parietal cortex is damaged, very bizarre perceptions and reactions occur, such as ignoring one side of your body because you think it is a stranger.

The limbic system consists of the hippocampus, the rim of cortex on the inside of the halves around the corpus callosum called the *cingulate cortex*, and two almond-shaped heads near the frontal region, each one called the *amygdala*. This set of structures is the closest thing to what Freud referred to as the id, the seat of emotion and animal drive. It is the older region of the cortex in terms of evolution and is also involved in memory.

Strange things can happen when the cortex is damaged. (A great book on this subject is *The Man Who Mistook His Wife for a Hat*, by Dr. Oliver Sacks.) I find this particularly fascinating because it means that who you are as a person in terms of identity and interaction with other people depends completely on the complex and precise interaction of all these neural areas. It suggests that your identity depends on your neurology and not merely on a spirit living in your body.

Social Phobias

Social phobias are distinguished by specific fears of social or performance situations, especially where there is potential for loss of face, embarrassment, or causing worry to others present. Social phobics resist leading meetings, taking oral examinations, making presentations, picking up new people at the airport or train station, going to cocktail parties, and attending social functions for civil or religious groups.

In his 1998 Broadway show, comedian Jerry Seinfeld cited a study that found that the number one fear of people surveyed was public speaking, with the fear of death coming in as the number two fear. "That means," Seinfeld observed, "given the choice, most people attending a funeral would prefer to be lying in the casket than up giving the eulogy!"

An estimated 10 million Americans suffer from social phobia (also known as social anxiety disorder). It is the most common anxiety disorder and the third most common psychiatric disorder after alcohol/substance abuse and depression.

Dr. David Sheehan, Professor of Psychiatry at the University of South Florida College of Medicine, emphasizes that social phobia "...is not shyness; people with this condition are profoundly disabled and significantly cost-burdened....People with this condition have fewer social skills, than, let's say, you would find in panic disorder patients, who tend to cling to other people. So as a result, these anxious patients are more likely to get depressed. They're also less likely to marry people who don't have a social anxiety disorder. They're more likely to drop out of school early, be unemployed, and not seek work. They have difficulty interviewing for jobs, and they're likely to turn down promotions. They usually have fewer friends, and tend to cling to friends who might mistreat them....They are so anxious about meeting new people that they assume it's safer to stick with what they have regardless of whether the relationship is healthy or ideal. They tend to refrain from dating and are more likely to live with their parents as adults."

In certain cultures, including Japan and Korea, individuals with social phobia may develop an excessive fear of giving offense to others rather than of being embarrassed themselves. They may have extreme anxiety that eye-to-eye contact, blushing, or one's body odor will be offensive to others.

Typically, social phobia starts in the midteens. Onset may come slowly or may be abrupt after a stressful or humiliating experience. In adulthood, social phobia may come on quickly following a particularly traumatic performance situation, such as a public speaking experience that did not go well.

✎✎✎

While it may not be evident at first, you'll soon see how *skimming* can save you a lot of reading time. Even if a more in-depth reading is necessary, you will find that by having gone through this process, you will have developed the kind of skeletal framework that will make your further reading faster, easier, and more meaningful. And if all you need is "just the facts, ma'am," your ability to *scan* a selection, chapter, or book will save you minutes, if not hours, every week.

Whether you're skimming or scanning, you will have equipped yourself with the ability to better digest what it is the author is trying to communicate.

CHAPTER 5

The Challenge of Technical Texts

 OU'VE ALREADY LEARNED a lot of ways to improve your reading. It's time to examine the unique challenges posed by highly technical texts. Physics, trigonometry, chemistry, calculus—you know, subjects that three-fourths of all students avoid like the plague. Even those students who manage to do well in such subjects wouldn't dare call them "easy-A" courses.

More than any other kind of reading, these subjects demand a logical, organized approach and a step-by-step reading method.

And they require a detection of the text's *organizational devices.*

Developing the skill to identify the basic sequence of the text will enable you to follow the progression of thought, a progression that is vital to your comprehension and retention.

Why? In most technical writing, each concept is like a building block of understanding—if you don't understand a particular section or concept, you won't be able to understand the *next* section either.

Most technical books are saturated with ideas, terms, formulas, and theories. The chapters are dense with information, compressing a great wealth of ideas into a small space. They demand to be read very carefully.

In order to get as much as possible from such reading assignments, you can take advantage of some devices to make sense of the organization. Here are five basics to watch for:

1. Definitions and terms.
2. Examples.
3. Classifications and listings.
4. Comparison and contrast.
5. Cause-effect relationships.

As you read any text, but certainly a highly specialized one, identifying these devices will help you grasp the main idea, as well as any details that are essential to your thorough understanding of the material.

Definitions and terms

In reading any specialized text, you must begin at the beginning—understanding the terms particular to that discipline. Familiar, everyday words have very precise definitions in technical writing.

What do I mean? Take the word *nice*. You may compliment your friend's new sweater, telling her it's *nice*, meaning attractive. You may find that the new chemistry teacher is *nice*, meaning he doesn't give too much homework. And when your friend uses the word *nice* to describe the blind date she's set up for you, it may mean something completely different—and insidious.

Everyday words can have a variety of meanings, some of them even contradictory, depending on the context in which they're used.

In contrast, in the sciences, terminology has fixed and specific meanings. For example, the definition of elasticity— *"the ability of a solid to regain its shape after a deforming force has been applied"*—is the same in Bangkok, Borneo, or Brooklyn. Such exact terminology enables scientists to communicate with the precision their discipline requires.

Definitions may vary in length. One term may require a one-sentence definition; others merit entire paragraphs. Some may even need a whole chapter to accurately communicate the definition.

Examples

A second communication tool is the example. Authors use examples to bridge abstract principles to concrete illustrations. These examples are essential to your ability to comprehend intricate and complicated theories.

Unlike other writing, technical writing places a very high premium on brevity. Economizing words is the key to covering a large volume of knowledge in a relatively small space. Few technical texts or articles include anecdotal matter or chatty stories of the author's experience.

This fact challenges the reader to pay particular attention to the examples that are included. Why? Technical writing often is filled with new or foreign ideas—many of which are not readily digestible. They are difficult in part because they are abstract. Examples work to clarify these concepts, hopefully in terms more easily understood.

For example, it may be difficult for you to make sense of the definition of symbiosis—"*the living together of two dissimilar organisms, especially when mutually beneficial*" — but the example of the bird that picks food from the crocodile's teeth, thereby feeding itself and keeping the crocodile cavity-free, helps bring it home.

Classifications and listings

A third tool frequently utilized in texts is classifications and listings. Classifying is the process by which common subjects are categorized under a general heading:

There are four seasons: winter, spring, summer, and fall.

Classification: seasons

Listing: winter, spring, summer, fall

There are four time zones in the United States: Eastern, Central, Mountain, and Pacific.

Classification: U.S. time zones

Listing: Eastern, Central, Mountain, Pacific

Especially in technical writing, authors use classification to categorize extensive lists of detail. Such writings may have several categories and subcategories that organize these details in some manageable fashion.

Comparing/contrasting

A fourth tool used in communicating difficult information is that of comparing and contrasting. Texts use this tool to bring complicated material into focus by offering a similar or opposing picture.

Such devices are invaluable in grasping concepts that do not conjure a picture in your mind. Gravity, for example, is not something that can be readily pictured — it's not a tangible object that can be described.

Through comparison, a text relates a concept to one that has been previously defined — or to one a reader may readily understand. Through contrast, the text concentrates on the differences and distinctions between two ideas. By focusing on distinguishing features, these ideas become clearer as one idea is held up against another.

Cause-effect relationships

A final tool that texts employ to communicate is the cause-effect relationship. This device is best defined in the context of science, where it is the fundamental quest of most scientific research.

Science begins with the observation of the effect — what is happening? It is snowing.

The next step is to conduct research into the cause: _Why_ is it snowing? Detailing this cause-effect relationship is often the essence of scientific and technical writing.

Cause-effect relationships may be written in many ways. The effect may be stated first, followed by the cause. An effect may be the result of several connected causes — a causal chain. And a cause may have numerous effects.

In your reading, it is vital that you recognize this relationship and its significance.

Read with a plan

More than any other type of writing, highly specialized, technical writing must be read with a plan. You can't approach your reading assignment merely with the goal of completing it. Such mindless reading will leave you confused and frustrated, drowning in an ocean of theory, concepts, terms, and examples.

Your plan should incorporate the following guidelines:

1. **Learn the terms** that are essential to understanding the concepts presented. Knowing the precise definitions that the author uses will enable you to follow his chain of thought through the text.

2. **Determine the structure or organization of the text.** Most chapters have a definite pattern that forms the skeleton of the material. A book may begin with a statement of a theory, give examples, provide sample problems, then summarize. Often this pattern can be discerned through a preview of the table of contents or the titles and subtitles.

3. **Skim the chapter** to get a sense of the author's viewpoint. Ask questions to define your purpose in reading. Use any summaries or review questions to guide your reading.

4. **Do a thorough analytical reading** of the text. Do not proceed from one section to the next until you have a clear understanding of the section you are reading—the concepts generally build upon each other. To proceed to a new section without understanding the ones that precede it is, at best, futile.

5. **Immediately upon concluding your thorough reading, review!** Write a summary of the concepts and theories you need to remember. Answer any questions raised when you skimmed the text. Do the problems. If possible, apply the formulas.

Technical material is saturated with ideas. When reading it, you must be convinced of one fact: Every individual word counts! You will want to read such material with the utmost concentration—it is not meant to be sped through.

Good readers know that such material demands a slow read that concentrates on achieving the greatest level of retention.

✎ Every definition has to be digested.

✎ Every formula must be committed to memory.

✎ Every example needs to be considered.

To improve your reading of such technical material, you will want to hone the skill of identifying the devices an author uses to communicate. In so doing, you will be able to connect the chain of thought that occurs. When reading such texts — or attempting to work out technical problems — try the following "tricks":

✎ Whenever you can, "translate" formulas and numbers into words. To test your understanding, try to put your translation into *different* words.

✎ Even if you're not particularly visual, pictures can often help. You should try translating a particularly vexing math problem into a drawing or diagram.

✎ Before you even get down to solving a problem, is there any way for you to estimate the answer or, at least, to estimate the range within which the answer should fall (greater than one, but less than 10)? This is the easy way to make sure you wind up in the right ballpark.

✎ Play around. There are often different paths to the same solution, or even equally valid solutions. If you find one, try to find others. This is a great way to increase your understanding of all the principles involved.

✎ When you are checking your calculations, try working *backwards*. I've found it the easiest way to catch simple mathematical errors.

✎ Try to figure out what is being asked, what principles are involved, what information is important, and what is not.

✎ Teach someone else. Trying to explain mathematical concepts to someone else will quickly pinpoint what you really know or don't know. It's virtually impossible to get someone else—especially someone who is slower than you at all this stuff—to understand if you don't!

CHAPTER 6

Becoming a Critical Reader

FTER FOUR YEARS of undergraduate work, before my dear alma mater would award me the degree for which I felt my dollars, sweat, and blood had amply paid, I was made to endure a six-hour essay test. We literature majors were given one question—"Analyze and interpret the following:" (the "following" being a poem we had never seen before...and several blue books in which to write our erudite answers).

Unbelievable?

Hardly!

This test was given in much the same way that the Educational Testing Service gives their PSAT, SAT, ACT, LSAT,GRE, and GMAT verbal tests. In the notorious reading comprehension section, you are required to read a distilled passage — which, unless you've stolen a peek at the exam, you have never seen — and then given four to six questions to determine if you have any clue as to what you just read.

You will find that there are many times, particularly in comparative literature classes, when you will need to read something with great care in order to remember details and interpret meaning. Hester Prynne's red monogram, Poe's talking raven, and Samuel Beckett's mysterious friend all require a little more analysis than a superficial interpretation of props and plot.

Yet such detailed, analytical reading is not limited to literature. Political dissertations, historical analyses, and even scientific research may require more careful reading than the latest "space opera."

Such reading is often referred to as *critical reading,* a type of reading during which you seek to distinguish thoughts, ideas, or concepts — each demanding thorough study and evaluation.

Critical reading requires that you are able to identify the author's arguments, measure their worth and truth, and apply what is pertinent to your own experience. Unlike skimming, critical reading challenges the reader to concentrate at the highest level possible.

Prepare yourself to read critically

When preparing to read critically, you must lay the groundwork for concentration. Just as an athlete must ready himself mentally to achieve peak performance, you will want to ready yourself before you begin to read.

To prepare to read critically:

1. You must have a clearly defined purpose for reading. Make sure that you've identified your purpose before you begin.

2. Pay attention! Avoid letting your mind wander to that conversation you and your friend had today at lunch. Minimize distractions and interruptions — anything or anyone that causes you to break your focus.

3. Find your optimum study environment — a quiet corner in the library, your own room, wherever. In absolute silence, or with your new CD playing. (Be sure to read _Manage Your Time_ or _Get Organized,_ two of the books in my _How to Study Program,_ for more tips on finding _your_ perfect study environment.)

4. Do not concern yourself with how fast or slowly you read. Your goal should be to understand the material, not to find out how fast you can get through it.

5. If it seems that you will need several hours to complete your reading, you might break the longer assignments into smaller, more manageable parts, then reward yourself at the end of each of these sections by taking brief breaks.

If you take these steps prior to reading any text that requires your utmost concentration, you will find that your mind is readied for the kind of focus necessary to read critically. Make a _habit_ of such preparations, and you will set yourself up to succeed.

Prereading is a must

Once you have prepared your mind to read, the next step is to understand the big picture — what is the author's thesis or main idea? Good comprehension is the consequence of your ability to grasp the main point of what the author is trying to communicate.

And grasping this message is accomplished through skimming the text, as we discussed in Chapter 4. Let's review the basic steps:

1. If there is a title or heading, rephrase it as a question. This will support your purpose for reading.

2. Examine all subheadings, illustrations, and graphics, as these will help you identify the significant matter within the text.

3. Read the introductory paragraphs, summary, and any questions at the end of the chapter.

4. Read the first sentence of every paragraph. In Chapter 3 you learned that this is generally where the main idea is found.

5. Evaluate what you have gained from this process: Can you answer the questions at the chapter's end? Could you intelligently participate in a class discussion of the material?

6. Write a brief summary of what you have learned from your skimming.

By beginning critical reading with a 20-minute skim of the text, you should be ready to answer three questions:

1. What is the text's principal message or viewpoint?

2. Is an obvious chain of thought or reasoning revealed?

3. What major points are addressed?

Now, *read* it

Once you identify and understand the basic skeleton of the material, your actual "read" of the material—following the details, reasoning, and chain of thought—is simply a matter of attaching meat to the bones.

This digestive process involves learning to interpret and evaluate what is written, what is directly stated, and what can be inferred from the context.

Effective analytical reading requires that you, the reader, distinguish the explicit, literal meaning of words *(denotation)* and what suggestions or intentions are intimated by the general content *(connotation)*.

Analyzing: What the words *connote*

Words and writing have two levels of meaning that are important to the reader's comprehension.

The first level is the literal or descriptive meaning. What a word expressly *denotes* means the specific, precise definition you'd find in the dictionary.

Connotation involves this second level of meaning — that which incorporates the total *significance* of the words.

What does that mean? Beyond a literal definition, words communicate emotion, bias, attitude, and perspective. Analyzing any text involves learning to interpret what is implied, just as much as what is expressly stated.

15 questions to help you

Beyond grasping the meaning of words and phrases, critical reading requires that you ask questions. Here are 15 questions that will help you effectively analyze and interpret most of what you read.

1. Is there a clear message communicated throughout?
2. Are the relationships between the points direct and clear?
3. Is there a relationship between your experience and the author's?

4. Are the details factual?
5. Are the examples and evidence relevant?
6. Is there consistency of thought?
7. What is the author's bias or slant?
8. What is the author's motive?
9. What does the author want you to believe?
10. Does this jibe with your own beliefs or experiences?
11. Is the author rational or subjective?
12. Is there a confusion between feelings and facts?
13. Are the main points logically ordered?
14. Are the arguments and conclusions consistent?
15. Are the explanations clear?

Obviously, this list of questions is not all-inclusive, but it will give you a jump start when critical reading is required. Remember, the essential ingredient to any effective analysis and interpretation is the questions you ask.

Summarizing: The final step

Nothing will be more important to your recall than learning to condense what you read into a clear and concise summary.

Many of you have learned to do this by excerpting entire segments or sentences from a text, certainly not a very efficient method for summarizing.

I recommend using the traditional outline (which is explained in detail in *Take Notes*, another of the books in the *How to Study Program*).

Another suggestion is to use a two-step process called *diagramming*, which calls for you to *diagram* or illustrate the content you've just read, then write a brief synopsis of what you've learned.

Similar to outlining, diagramming helps you to visualize the relationships between various thoughts and ideas. Concept diagrams, or concept trees, are very useful visual aids for depicting the structure of a textbook.

Unless you have a photographic memory, you will find that recalling a picture of the main points will greatly increase what you remember. Beyond this, such diagrams require that you distill what is essential to the text and how it relates to the main message.

Suppose you read a chapter in your language arts class about the types of sciences. Your diagram might reduce your reading material to look like the following:

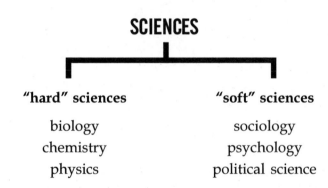

More than a listing of main points, a diagram allows you to picture how parts fit together, which enhances your ability to recall the information you've read. This is especially true the more "visual" you are.

Distill it into a synopsis

The second step in the process of summarizing is to write a brief synopsis of what you've learned. When you need to review the material, diagrams will remind you of the significant elements in the text. Your synopsis will remind you of the main idea.

The goal here is to put in your own words what you gleaned from what you read. You will find this process an invaluable gauge of whether you have understood the message — and on what level.

Use this method one chapter at a time:

1. Write definitions of any key terms you feel are essential to understanding the topic.
2. Write questions and answers you feel clarify the topic.
3. Write any questions for which you don't have answers — then make sure you find them through rereading, further research, or asking another student or your teacher.
4. Even if you still have unanswered questions, move on to the next section and complete numbers one to three for that section. (And so on, until your reading assignment is complete.) See if this method doesn't help you get a better handle on any assignment right from the start.

Critical reading is not easy. It requires a lot more concentration and effort than the quick-reference reading that you can get away with for much of your day-to-day class assignments. And I won't kid you — much of the reading you'll do in the latter years of high school and throughout college will be critical reading.

But if you follow the steps I've outlined for each critical reading assignment that you tackle — preparing yourself for the read, doing a preread skim followed by an analytical reading, concluding with a summarization — you'll discover that critical reading can be a much smoother, even rewarding, experience!

The method you probably learned

If you were taught a specific reading method in school, it was probably the one developed back in the 1940s that is abbreviated "SQ3R." This stands for **S**urvey, **Q**uestion, **R**ead, **R**ecite, and **R**eview. Here's how the process works:

Survey. Preread the chapter, concentrating on topic sentences, subheads, and review questions, in order to get an overview of what's ahead.

Question. Once you've surveyed the chapter, ask yourself what information is contained in it. Consider turning the subheads into questions as an exercise.

Read. Now read the first section thoroughly, attempting to answer the questions you've posed. Take notes, highlight, underline, map.

Recite. Now answer the questions *without* looking at your notes or the text. When you're done, go on to the next section. Continue this detailed reading/reciting tandem until you finish the chapter (or the assignment).

Review. Go back over the entire assignment.

Does this sound familiar? I agree. I think this method is completely incorporated into the steps I've outlined in this and previous chapters. Frankly, I think the detailed method I've proposed — and the helpful advice along the way — covers far more ground.

CHAPTER 7

Reading the Literature

"WILL YOU WALK *a little faster?" said a whiting to a snail.*

"There's a porpoise close behind us and he's treading on my tail!"

"If I'd been the whiting," said Alice, whose thoughts were still running on the song, "I'd have said to the porpoise, 'Keep back, please; we don't want you with us!' "

"They were obliged to have him with them," the Mock Turtle said. "No wise fish would go anywhere without a Porpoise."

"Wouldn't it really?" said Alice in a tone of great surprise.

"Of course not," said the Mock Turtle. "Why, if a fish came to me, and told me he was going on a journey, I should say, 'With what porpoise?' "

"Don't you mean 'purpose?' " said Alice.
"I mean what I say," the Mock Turtle replied in an offended tone.
— Lewis Carroll, *Alice in Wonderland*

✎✎✎

In this excerpt, you could enjoy the nonsensical picture of a porpoise forcing a snail and whiting to walk faster. You might laugh at the confusion of "porpoise" and "purpose" by the Mock Turtle. Or you could discern the *message* — that you need to have a purpose when you are on a journey...or reading.

In today's world of the Sega Dreamcast, the WWF, and the Dave Matthews Band, literature often takes a back seat. So much so that many of your classmates (not *you*, of course) may not even know that *Alice in Wonderland* is an important piece of literature.

Why should you care about literature? Who needs to read the book when you can see the movie?

While I didn't write this book to give you a lecture on the merits of the classics, please bear with me for a couple of paragraphs.

The greatest involvement device

Unlike anything else, literature *involves* the reader in the story. How? There are no joysticks to manipulate, no SurroundSound to engulf you. Your imagination is your only involvement device, but it far surpasses any high-tech computer gimmicks.

Your imagination makes reading the ultimate adventure. It allows you to immerse yourself in the story — identifying with the protagonist, fighting his battles, experiencing his fears, sharing his victories. You may become so involved, you end up staying up well past your bedtime, turning page after page late into the night!

Your imagination is the vehicle that allows you to explore a million different lives, from floating down the Mississippi River on a raft, to suffering through a star-crossed love affair, to having tea with the March Hare and the Mad Hatter, as our Alice did.

Creative writing may be serious or humorous or sublime...or all three. It is often subtle; meanings are elusive and delicate. Such writing, when done effectively, evokes emotional responses. You get angry. You shed a tear. You chuckle. An author's expression strikes a chord that moves you. You and the author communicate on a level that is far beyond an exchange of facts and information.

Enough said. Assuming that I have converted all you literature skeptics to avid library loiterers (and even if I haven't), I'll offer some advice to help you begin your journey to literary appreciation. It begins with understanding the basic road map.

Which reading method: pleasure or critical?

While I certainly encourage you to approach your reading with the enthusiasm and anticipation that would justify the pleasure-reading method (see Chapter 2), the demands of your teacher who assigns the reading will probably require the *critical* reading method.

Reading literature requires most of the skills we've discussed previously.

There are devices and clues to ferret out that will help you follow the story and understand its meaning better.

You will analyze and interpret what the author is saying and evaluate its worth.

But in addition, in literature, you will be able to appreciate the *words* themselves. In textbooks, you often must penetrate a thick jungle of tangled sentences and murky paragraphs to find the information you seek.

Great literature _is_ its language. It's the flow and ebb of its words, the cadence of its sentences, as much as it is story and theme.

As you read more, you'll uncover the diversity of tapestries that different authors weave with words. You may discover similar themes coursing through the works of authors like Ernest Hemingway or Thomas Hardy, but their use of language is as different as desert and forest. The composition of the words themselves is an element you'll want to examine as you critically read literature.

Fiction: Just another word for storytelling

Most fiction is an attempt to tell a story. There is a _beginning,_ in which the characters and the setting are introduced. There is a _conflict or struggle_ (middle) that advances the story to a _climax_ (end), where the conflict is resolved. A final _denouement_ or "winding up" clarifies the conclusion of the story.

Your literature class will address all of these parts using literary terms that are often more confusing than helpful. The following are brief definitions of some of the more important ones:

Plot. The order or sequence of the story—how it proceeds from the opening through the climax. Your ability to understand and appreciate literature depends upon how well you follow the plot—the _story._

Characterization. The personalities or characters central to the story—the heroes, heroines, and villains. You will want to identify the main characters of the story and their relationship to the struggle or conflict. Pay particular attention as to whether the characters are three dimensional—are they real and believable?

Theme. The controlling message or subject of the story; the moral or idea that the author is using the plot and characters to communicate. Some examples: man's inhumanity to man, man's impotency in his environment, the corrupting influence of power, greed, and unrequited love. Just as with nonfiction, you need to discern this theme to really understand what it is the author wants to communicate.

Setting. The time and place in which the story takes place. This is especially important when reading a historical novel or one that takes you to another culture.

Point of view. Who is telling the story? Is it one of the central characters giving you flashbacks or a first-person perspective? Or is it a third-person narrator offering commentary and observations on the characters, the setting, and the plot? This person moves the story along and gives it an overall tone.

The first step in reading literature is to familiarize yourself with these concepts and then try to recognize them in each novel or short story you read.

The second step is the same as for reading nonfiction—to identify your purpose for reading.

Allow your purpose to define how you will read. If you are reading to be entertained, then a pleasure read is the way to go. If you're reading for a class and will be required to participate in discussions or be tested on the material, you'll want to do a critical read.

How long should it take?

As a general rule, fiction is not meant to be read over a period of months—or even weeks. Try to read it as quickly as possible to get a full appreciation of the author's plot, characters, and theme. You should read fast enough to progress through the plot, get a sense of the characters and their struggles, and discern the author's message or theme.

It's helpful to set a goal as to when you want to finish your reading. Frequently, of course, this will already be set for you, if your reading is a class assignment.

You should, however, set daily goals. Set aside one or two hours to read, or set a goal of reading three chapters a day until you finish. Reading sporadically — 10 minutes one day, a half hour the next, then not picking up the book until several days later — means that you'll lose track of the plot and characters and just as quickly lose interest.

Too often when students do not establish a regular schedule, their reading becomes fragmented, making it very difficult to piece together the whole story. A reasonable goal is to try to read a novel in less than a week, a short story in one sitting. To achieve this goal, once you begin, you should read every day until you finish. By doing this, the story and characters will stay fresh in your mind.

If you try to read fiction more rapidly, you will greatly increase your enjoyment of it. It is vitally important that as you try to read faster, you give the story your full attention. By doing this you will be surprised by how improved your understanding and appreciation are.

To speed your reading of fiction, try this experiment:

1. Find a novel or short story that interests you and is relatively easy to read. Tomes like _Ulysses_ or _Naked Lunch_ shouldn't be candidates.
2. Set aside two or three hours to invest in reading the book. If at all possible, finish it in one sitting. If you can't, then allocate the same amount of time each day until you do.

By trying this experiment, you will discover that fiction is _intended_ to be read this way — in one sitting, whenever possible. It is as if you are sitting at a master storyteller's feet as he spins his tale. You want to know how the story ends and what happens to the hero.

Will the villain get his comeuppance? Will the hero get the girl? Or ride off with his horse?

You'll find that you appreciate the story far more at the end than anywhere in the middle.

Some other tips for reading fiction:

1. Understand the plot and maintain awareness of its progression.
2. Take breaks to review what has occurred and who is involved.
3. Vary your reading method—from skimming transitional bridge material to carefully reading description and narration.
4. Question the story's theme. What is the message?

You're allowed to enjoy it

A final recommendation: Give yourself permission to *enjoy* what you are reading. You will be amazed at the difference this will make. Fiction, unlike any other reading, can take you on an adventure. Through your mind, you can journey to faraway lands, pretend you are someone else, feel emotions you may never otherwise experience. All this happens as you gain an appreciation of literature—as you learn to understand fiction and allow yourself to enjoy great stories.

CHAPTER 8

Focusing Your Mind

ONCENTRATION. IT'S ONE of the biggest challenges facing any reader.

Why? Unlike other activities, reading requires an *active* mind and a *passive* body. A deadly combination, especially when you've spent the day in classes and haven't had a chance to burn off that excess energy with a tennis match, a game of "hoops," or a quick run around campus.

Concentration-wise, reading can be more demanding than class lectures, homework assignments, or note-taking. In class, you at least have vocal variety and the threat of being called on to keep you focused. And writing, while a sedentary activity, still requires some hand-eye coordination to keep your brain working.

Keep your mind on one thing

Concentration begins with the ability to keep your mind focused on one thing—your reading assignment. This is not an innate talent, but a learned discipline. Much like an athlete must learn to be so focused that she is completely unaffected by the screaming crowds, a good reader becomes absorbed in what he's reading.

How does *your* mind discipline "rate"? Answer these questions to find out:

1. When I read, do I often allow random thoughts to steal my focus?
2. As I read, am I easily distracted by noises or other activities?
3. Am I watching the clock to see how long I have been reading?

There is no simple, magic formula for conjuring up concentration—especially when you're faced with a critical reading assignment you're not particularly looking forward to. But if you follow the preparatory steps I've discussed in previous chapters—define your purpose, skim for a preread, identify questions for which you will seek answers—you should find it a bit easier to stay focused.

Steps to better concentration

Here are some other practical steps I recommend to increase your ability to concentrate:

1. **Get some exercise** before you begin your reading. A game of racquetball, an exercise class, a workout at the gym, even a brisk walk, will help burn off *physical* energy so you'll be able to direct all of your *mental* energy to your reading.

2. **Read in the right place.** No, it's not in front of the TV, nor in your room if your roommate is hosting a pizza party. Reading is a solitary activity. Find a quiet corner, preferably in a place designated for study only—at your desk or in the library. Although tempting, reading on your bed can be dangerous if you're struggling to concentrate. You just may lose the battle and find yourself in the perfect place to doze off.

3. **Eliminate distractions.** If you've properly scheduled your reading time (see **Get Organized**), you won't be distracted by other pending assignments. If you're trying to read one assignment while worrying about another, your concentration—and comprehension—will inevitably suffer.

   Make sure there's nothing else in sight to vie for your attention. Are there letters on your desk that you need to answer? Put them away and schedule some time to write back. Sirens and screams from the TV show in the other room? Turn it off or down or, better yet, close your door.

4. **Plan breaks.** If you have three hours or more of reading ahead of you, the mere thought of it may be so discouraging that you'll lose your concentration before you even pick up the book. Schedule short 10- or 15-minute breaks after each hour of reading. Get up. Listen to some music. Stretch. If you must break more frequently, keep your breaks shorter. By breaking up your reading into smaller, more digestible bites, you'll be able to concentrate more effectively.

Wait! Don't start reading yet.

Have you defined your purpose for reading? Once again, you must have a clearly defined purpose or goal. What are you reading for? (I have addressed this numerous times, but spaced repetition is a very effective way to make a point.)

The point is that reading without purpose is the greatest means to getting nowhere, which is where you'll find your mind after about a half-hour.

Know why you are reading. If your teacher or professor has given you questions to answer, then you know what you're looking for. If not, ask your *own* questions, using the clues in your book (as discussed in Chapter 2).

An effective preread of the material should help you define your purpose and stimulate some interest in finding out more—which will result in increased concentration.

Motivation: Crucial to concentration

Motivation is key to your success in just about any endeavor, whether it's graduating with honors, maintaining an effective time-management program, or improving your reading. You can utilize all the tricks and steps I've mentioned in this chapter, but if you lack the motivation to read, you'll still find it a struggle to concentrate on your assignments.

There are two types of motivation—intrinsic and extrinsic. What's the difference?

An avid murder mystery fan, you buy stacks of paperbacks at the used bookstore and spend your free time with your nose buried in them. You love the challenge of figuring out who's guilty before you reach the end. In fact, you'd spend all weekend reading mysteries if you didn't have to complete a reading assignment for your political science class. You're not particularly interested in poly sci, but your efforts on this assignment could secure you an A for the term, so you're determined to read the material and "ace" the exam.

Your motivation for reading the mysteries is intrinsic — you do it because you enjoy it. You don't get any awards. You don't get paid for it.

The poly sci reading, on the other hand, requires external motivation. You're reading it because you want to earn a high grade in class. Your reward is external — beyond the reading itself.

Whether you are intrinsically motivated to read or doing it for some external reward doesn't matter as much as the fact that you are motivated by something! If you find it difficult to get excited about reading your economics assignment, remind yourself of how this exercise will help your grade — get yourself externally motivated.

If _that_ doesn't get you motivated enough to read for three hours, there's nothing wrong with a little bribery. Reward yourself with something more immediate. Promise yourself that if you stay focused on your reading until it's completed, you can rent the movie you've been wanting to see. Or you can buy that new CD. (Be careful, though. If you need _lots_ of extrinsic motivation, you could run out of money!)

The value of concentration can be summed up in one statement: Concentration is essential to comprehension. Where there is failure to focus, there will be little or no understanding.

Without concentration, you will see only words on a page.

CHAPTER 9

Retaining the Information

THE ULTIMATE TEST of your comprehension is what you remember *after* you have finished your reading—what you walk away with.

As a student, most of your reading will be for classes in which, sooner or later, you'll be required to regurgitate the information you've read in some type of format—essay test; term paper; or multiple-choice, true-false, or fill-in-the-blank final.

So, beyond just being able to *complete* your reading assignments, you want to be sure you *remember* what you read.

All of you have probably had the experience of forgetting that important fact that made the difference between an A- and a B+ (or a B- and a C+). It was sitting right there, on the tip of your brain. But you couldn't quite remember it.

Memory *can* be improved

You probably know people with photographic (or near-photographic) memories. They know all the words to every song recorded in the last four years, remind you of things you said to them three years ago, and never forget anyone's birthday (or anniversary or "day we met" or "first kiss day," *ad infinitum*).

While some people seem to be able to retain information naturally, a good memory—like good concentration—*can* be learned. You can control what stays in your mind and what is forgotten. The key to this control is to learn and tap into the essential elements of good memory.

Some people remember with relative ease and have no problem retaining large volumes of information. Others often are aggravated by a faulty memory that seems to lose more than it retains. Several factors contribute to your capability to recall information you take in:

Intelligence, age, and experience all play a role in how well you remember. Not everyone remembers the same way. You need to identify how these factors affect your memory and learn to maximize your strengths.

Laying a strong foundation is important to good memory. Most learning is an addition to something you already know. If you never grasped basic chemistry, then mastering organic chemistry will be virtually impossible. By developing a broad base of basic knowledge, you will enhance your ability to recall new information.

Motivation is key to improving your memory. A friend of mine, the consummate baseball fan, seems to know every baseball statistic from the beginning of time. He can spout off batting averages and ERAs from any decade for virtually any player, his favorite team's season schedule...and most of the other teams', too! While I wouldn't say he is the most intelligent guy I've ever met, he obviously loves baseball and is highly motivated to memorize as much as possible about his favorite subject.

You probably have a pet interest, too. Whether it's movies, music, or sports, you've filled your brain with a mountain of information. Now, if you can learn that much about one subject, you are obviously capable of retaining information about other subjects—even chemistry. You just have to learn how to motivate yourself.

A method, system, or process for retaining information is crucial to increasing your recall. This may include organizing your thinking, good study habits, or mnemonic devices—some means that you utilize when you have to remember.

Using what you learn, soon after you learn it, is important to recall. It's fine to memorize a vocabulary list for a quick quiz, but if you wish to retain information for the long haul, you must reinforce your learning by using this knowledge. For example, you will add a new word to your permanent vocabulary if you make a point to use it, correctly, in a conversation.

The study of foreign languages, for many, proves frustrating when there are no opportunities outside of class to practice speaking the language. That's why foreign-language students often join conversation groups or study abroad— to reinforce retention of what they have learned by using it.

Why we forget

As you think about the elements of developing good memory, you can use them to address why you *forget*. The root of poor memory is usually found in one of these areas:

1. We fail to make the material meaningful.
2. We did not learn prerequisite material.
3. We fail to grasp what is to be remembered.
4. We do not have the desire to remember.

5. We allow apathy or boredom to dictate how we learn.
6. We have no set habit for learning.
7. We are disorganized and inefficient in our use of study time.
8. We do not use the knowledge we have gained.

All of us are inundated with information every day, bombarded with facts, concepts, and opinions. We are capable of absorbing some information simply because the media drench us with it. (I've never read Nancy Reagan's notorious unauthorized biography, nor do I intend to, but how could I not be aware of her reputation for recycling Christmas gifts?)

In order to retain most information, we have to make a concerted effort to do so. We must make this same effort with the material we read.

How to remember

There are some basic tools that will help you remember what you read:

Understanding. You will remember only what you understand. When you read something and grasp the message, you have begun the process of retention. The way to test this is to state the message in your own words. Can you summarize the main idea? Unless you understand what is being said, you won't be able to decide whether it is to be remembered or discarded.

Desire. Let me repeat: You remember what you *choose* to remember. If you do not want to retain some piece of information or don't believe you *can*, then you *won't*! To remember the material, you must *want* to remember it and be convinced that you *will* remember it.

Overlearn. To insure that you retain material, you need to go beyond simply doing the assignment. To really remember what you learn, you should learn material thoroughly, or *over*learn. This involves prereading the text, doing a critical read, and having some definite means of review that reinforces what you should have learned.

Systematize. It's more difficult to remember random thoughts or numbers than those organized in some pattern. For example, which phone number is easier to remember: 538-6284 or 678-1234? Once you recognize the pattern in the second number, it takes much less effort to remember than the first. You should develop the ability to discern the structure that exists and recall it when you try to remember. Have a system to help you recall how information is organized and connected.

Association. It's helpful to attach or associate what you are trying to recall to something you already have in your memory. Mentally link new material to existing knowledge so that you are giving this new thought some context in your mind.

If you take these principles and apply them to your reading assignment, you can develop a procedure that will increase what you take with you from your reading.

A procedure to improve recall

Each time you attempt to read something that you must recall, use this six-step process:

1. **Evaluate the material and define your purpose** for reading. Identify your interest level and get a sense of how difficult the material is.

2. **Choose appropriate reading techniques** for the purpose of your reading. If you are reading to grasp the main idea, that is what you will recall.

3. **Identify the important facts.** Remember what you need to. Identify associations that connect the details you must recall.

4. **Take notes.** Use your own words to give a synopsis of the main ideas. Use an outline, diagram, or concept tree to show relationships and patterns. Your notes provide an important backup to your memory. Writing down key points will further reinforce your ability to remember.

5. **Review.** Quiz yourself on those things you must remember. Develop some system by which you review notes at least three times before you are required to recall. The first review should be shortly after you've read, the second should come a few days later, and the final should take place just before you are expected to recall. This process will help you avoid cram sessions.

6. **Implement.** Find opportunities to *use* the knowledge you have gained. Study groups and class discussions are invaluable opportunities to implement what you've learned.

Memorizing and mnemonics

To this point, we have concentrated on the fundamentals of remembering and retention. There are some narrow methods that will help you recall a lot of specific facts. The first of these is memorization—the process of trying to recall information word-for-word.

Memorize only when you are required to remember something for a relatively short time—when you have a history quiz on battle dates, a chemistry test on specific formulas, or a vocabulary test in French.

When memorization is required, you should do whatever is necessary to impress the exact information on your mind. Repetition is probably the most effective method. Write down the information on a 3 x 5 card and use it as a flashcard. You must quiz yourself frequently to assure that you know the information perfectly.

A second technique for recalling lots of details is *mnemonics*. A mnemonic device is used to help recall large bits of information that may or may not be logically connected. Such mnemonics are invaluable when you must remember facts not arranged in a clear fashion, items that are quite complicated, or numerous items that are a part of a series.

One of the simplest methods is to try to remember just the first letter of a sequence. That's how Roy G. Biv (the colors of the spectrum, in order from left to right — red, orange, yellow, green, blue, indigo, violet) came about. Or **E**very **G**ood **B**oy **D**oes **F**ine, to remember the notes on the musical staff. Or, perhaps the simplest of all, **FACE**, to remember the notes in between. (The latter two work opposite of old Roy — using *words* to remember *letters*.) Of course, not many sequences work out so nicely. If you tried to memorize the signs of the zodiac with this method, you'd wind up with **A**ries, **T**aurus, **G**emini, **C**ancer, **L**eo, **V**irgo, **L**ibra, **S**corpio, **S**agittarius, **C**apricorn, **A**quarius, **P**isces. Many of you may be able to make a name or a place or something out of ATGCLVLSSCAP, but I can't!

One solution is to make up a simple sentence that uses the first letters of the list you're trying to remember as the first letters of each word. For example, **A** **T**all **G**iraffe **C**hewed **L**eaves **V**ery **L**ow, **S**ome **S**low **C**ows **A**t **P**lay.

Wait a minute! It's the same number of words. Why not just figure out some way to memorize the first set of words? What's better about the second set? A couple of things. First of all, it's easier to picture the giraffe and cow and what they're doing. Creating mental images is a very powerful way to remember almost anything. Second, because the words in our sentence bear some relationship to each other, they're much easier to remember. Go ahead, try it. See how long it takes you to memorize the sentence as opposed to all the signs. This method is especially easy when you remember some or all of the items but _don't_ remember their _order_.

Remember: Make your sentence(s) memorable to _you_. _Any_ sentence or series of words that helps you remember these letters will do. Here are just two more I created in a few seconds: **A** Tall **G**irl **C**alled **L**ovely **V**era **L**oved to **S**ip **S**odas from **C**ans **A**nd **P**lates. **A**ny **T**iny **G**erbil **C**ould **L**ove **V**enus. **L**ong **S**illy **S**nakes **C**ould **A**ll **P**ray. (Isn't it easy to make up memorably silly pictures in your head for these?)

You will find that in business or the classroom, mnemonic devices like this allow you to readily recall specific information that you need to retain for longer periods of time. They are used to remember chemical classifications, lines of music, and anatomical lists.

As effective as mnemonic devices are, don't try to create them for everything you have to remember. Why? To generate a device for everything you need to learn would demand more time than any one person has. And you just might have trouble _remembering_ all the devices you created to help you remember in the first place! Too _many_ mnemonics can make your retention more complicated and hinder effective recall.

Complex mnemonics are not very useful—they can be too difficult to memorize. When you choose to utilize a mnemonic, you should keep it simple so that it facilitates the quick recall you intended.

Many people complain that their mind is a sieve—everything they read slips through; they never remember anything. I hope you now are convinced that this is a _correctable_ problem. You don't have to be a genius to have good retention—you simply must be willing to work at gaining the skills that lead to proficient recall. As you master these skills, you will improve your reading by increasing your rate of retention.

CHAPTER 10

Let's Read Up on ADD

I COULD WRITE a book on ADD, which seems to be the "diagnosis of choice" for schoolkids these days.

Luckily, I don't have to. Thom Hartmann has already written an excellent one—*Attention Deficit Disorder: A Different Perception*—from which I have freely and liberally borrowed (with his permission) for this chapter.

Some definitions, please

What is ADD? It's probably easiest to describe as a person's difficulty in focusing on a single thing for any significant duration of time. People with ADD are generally easily distracted, impatient, impulsive, and often seek immediate gratification. They have poor listening skills and trouble doing "boring" jobs (like sitting quietly in class or, as adults, balancing a checkbook). "Disorganized" and "messy" are words that also come up often.

Hyperactivity, however, is more clearly defined as restlessness, resulting in excessive activity. Hyperactives are usually described as having "ants in their pants." ADHD, the first category recognized in medicine some 75 years ago, is a combination of hyperactivity and ADD.

According to the American Psychiatric Association, a person has ADHD if he or she meets eight or more of the following paraphrased criteria:

1. Can't remain seated if required to do so.
2. Is easily distracted by extraneous stimuli.
3. Focusing on a single task is difficult.
4. Frequently begins another activity without completing the first.
5. Fidgets or squirms (or feels restless mentally).
6. Can't (or doesn't want to) wait for his turn during group activities.
7. Will often interrupt with an answer before a question is completed.
8. Has problems with chore or job follow-through.
9. Can't play quietly easily.
10. Impulsively jumps into physically dangerous activities without weighing the consequences.
11. Easily loses things (pencils, tools, papers) necessary to complete school or work projects.
12. Interrupts others inappropriately.
13. Talks impulsively or excessively.
14. Doesn't seem to listen when spoken to.

Three caveats to keep in mind: The behaviors must have started before age 7, not represent another form of classifiable mental illness, and occur more frequently than in the average person of the same age.

Characteristics of people with ADD

Let's look at the characteristics generally ascribed to people with ADD in more detail:

Easily distracted. Since ADD people are constantly "scoping out" everything around them, focusing on a single item is difficult. Just try having a conversation with an ADD person while a television is on.

Short, but very intense, attention span. Though it can't be defined in terms of minutes or hours, anything ADD people find boring immediately loses their attention. Other projects may hold their rapt and extraordinarily intense attention for hours or days.

Disorganization. ADD children are often chronically disorganized — their rooms are messy, their desks are a shambles, their files incoherent. While people without ADD can be equally messy and disorganized, they can usually find what they are looking for; ADDers *can't*.

Distortions of time-sense. ADDers have an exaggerated sense of urgency when they're working on something and an exaggerated sense of boredom when they have nothing interesting to do.

Difficulty following directions. A new theory on this aspect holds that ADDers have difficulty processing auditory or verbal information. A major aspect of this difficulty involves the very-common reports of parents of ADD kids who say their kids love to watch TV and hate to read.

Daydreaming, falling into depressions, or having mood swings.

Take risks. ADDers seem to make faster decisions than non-ADDers. This is why Thom Hartmann and Wilson Harrell, former publisher of *Inc.* magazine and author of *For*

Entrepreneurs Only, conclude that the vast majority of successful entrepreneurs probably have ADD! They call them "Hunters," as opposed to the more staid "Farmer" types.

Easily frustrated and impatient. ADDers do not beat around the bush or suffer fools gladly. They are direct and to the point. When things aren't working, "Do something!" is the ADD rallying cry, even if that something is a bad idea.

Why do ADD kids have trouble in school?

First and foremost, says Thom Hartmann, it's because schools are set up for "Farmers" — sit at a desk, do what you're told, and watch and listen to the teacher. This is hell for "Hunters" with ADD. The bigger the class size, the worse it becomes. Kids with ADD, remember, are easily distracted, easily bored, easily turned off, always ready to move on.

What should you look for in a school setting to make it more palatable to an ADDer? What can you do at home to help your child (or yourself)? Hartmann has some solid answers.

✎ **Learning needs to be project- and experience-based**, providing more opportunities for creativity and shorter and smaller "bites" of information. Many "gifted" programs offer exactly such opportunities. The problem for many kids with ADD is that they've spent years in non-gifted, farmer-type classroom settings and may be labeled with underachieving behavior problems, effectively shut out of the programs virtually designed for them! Many parents report that children diagnosed as ADD, who failed miserably in public school, thrived in private school. Hartmann attributes this to the smaller classrooms, more individual attention with specific goal-setting, project-based learning, and similar methods common in such schools. These factors are just what make ADD kids thrive!

✎ **Create a weekly performance template** on which *both* teacher and parent chart the child's performance, positive and negative. "Creating such a larger-than-the-child system," claims Hartmann, "will help keep ADD children on task and on time."

✎ **Encourage special projects for extra credit.** Projects give ADDers the chance to learn in the mode that's most appropriate to them. They will also give such kids the chance to make up for the "boring" homework they sometimes simply can't make themselves do.

✎ **Stop labeling them as "disordered."** Kids react to labels, especially negative ones, even more than adults do. Saying "you have a deficit and a disorder" may be more destructive than useful.

✎ **Think twice about medication,** but don't discard it as an option. Hartmann has a very real concern about the long-term side effects of the drugs normally prescribed for ADDers. He also notes that they may well be more at risk to be substance-abusers as adults, so starting them on medication at a young age sends a very mixed message. On the other hand, if an ADD child cannot have his or her special needs met in a classroom, *not* medicating him or her may be a disaster. "The relatively unknown long-term risks of drug therapy," says Hartmann, "may be more than offset by the short-term benefits of improved classroom performance."

Specific suggestions about reading

✎ **Practice, practice, practice.** ADDers will tend to have trouble reading, preferring visual stimulation to the "boring" words. Turn off the TV.

Minimize time spent with Sony PlayStation or other such games. ADDers may well be extraordinarily focused on such visual input and stimulating games, but only to the detriment of their schoolwork. Where possible, though, utilize videos, computers, interactive multimedia and other forms of communication more attuned to ADDers to help them learn. There is a tremendous amount of educational software and CD-ROM material that may work better for ADDers than traditional printed books.

However, ADDers must obviously learn to read and practice reading. I would suggest finding a professional or a program to deal with your or your child's probable reading problems. Anything you can do to make reading more fun and interesting should be explored.

✎ **Break everything into specific goal units.** ADDers are very goal-oriented; as soon as they reach one, it's on to the next. Reestablishing very short-term, "bite-size" goals is essential. Make goals specific, definable, and measurable, and stick to only one priority at a time.

✎ **Create distraction-free zones.** Henry David Thoreau (who evidently suffered from ADD, by the way) was so desperate to escape distraction he moved to isolated Walden Pond. Have them organize their time and workspace to create their own "Walden Pond," especially when they have to read, write, take notes, or study. ADDers need silence, so consider the library. Another tip: Have them clean their work area thoroughly at the end of each day. This will minimize distractions as they try to read.

✎ **Train your attention span.** ADDers will probably never be able to train themselves to ignore

distractions totally, but a variety of meditation techniques might help them stay focused longer.

✎ **Utilize short-term rewards.** ADD salespeople don't do well when a sales contest lasts for six months, even if the reward is, say, a 10-day cruise. But stick a $100 bill on the wall and watch them focus! Those with ADD are not motivated by rewards that are too ephemeral or too far in the future. They live for the here and now and need to be rewarded immediately.

CHAPTER 11

Build Your Own Library

> The reading of all good books is like conversation with the finest men of past centuries.
>
> —Descartes

 F YOU ARE ever to become an active, avid reader, access to books will do much to cultivate the habit. I suggest you "build" your own library. Your selections can and should reflect your own tastes and interests, but try to make them wide and varied. Include some of the classics, contemporary fiction, poetry, and biography.

Save your high school and college texts—especially those from any English composition or writing classes. You'll be amazed at how some of the material retains its relevance. And try to read a good newspaper every day so as to keep current and informed.

Your local librarian can refer you to any number of lists of the "great books," most of which are available in inexpensive paperback editions. Here are four more lists—compiled by yours truly—of "great" classical authors; "great" not-so-classical authors, poets, and playwrights; some contemporary "pretty greats"; and a selection of my own "great" books.

You may want to incorporate these on your buy list, especially if you're planning a summer reading program.

I'm sure that I have left off someone's favorite author or "important" title from these lists. So be it. They are not meant to be comprehensive, just relatively representative. I doubt anyone would disagree that a person familiar with the majority of authors and works listed would be considered well-read!

Who are Derek Walcott, Kenzaburo Oe, Nadine Gordimer, Octavio Paz, and Camilo Jose Cela? All winners of the Nobel Prize for Literature (1989 to 1994, plus Toni Morrison in 1993). I'm willing to bet a year's royalties not one of you reading this has heard of more than one of them (with the exception of Ms. Morrison). So how do *you* define great if these award winners are so anonymous? I include this merely to dissuade another 200 or so letters castigating me for those authors or works I *did* include in these lists.

Some "great" classical authors

Aeschylus	Chaucer
Aesop	Cicero
Aquinas	Confucius
Aristophanes	Dante
Aristotle	Descartes
Balzac	Dewey
Boccaccio	Emerson
Burke	Erasmus
Cervantes	Flaubert

Goethe

Hegel

Homer

Horace

J. Caesar

Kant

Machiavelli

Milton

Montaigne

Nietzsche

Ovid

Pindar

Plato

Plutarch

Rousseau

S. Johnson

Santayana

Shakespeare

Spinoza

Swift

Vergil

Voltaire

Some other "great" authors

Sherwood Anderson

W.H. Auden

Jane Austen

Samuel Beckett

Brandan Behan

William Blake

Bertolt Brecht

Charlotte Brontë

Emily Brontë

Pearl Buck

Samuel Butler

Lord Byron

Albert Camus

Lewis Carroll

Joseph Conrad

e.e cummings

Daniel Defoe

Charles Dickens

Emily Dickinson

John Dos Passos

Feodor Dostoevski

Arthur Conan Doyle

Theodore Dreiser

Alexandre Dumas

Lawrence Durrell

George Eliot

T.S. Eliot

William Faulkner

Edna Ferber

F. Scott Fitzgerald

Ford Madox Ford

E.M. Forster

Robert Frost	Vladimir Nabokov
John Galsworthy	O. Henry
Jose Ortega y Gasset	Eugene O'Neill
Nikolai Gogol	George Orwell
Maxim Gorki	Dorothy Parker
Thomas Hardy	Edgar Allan Poe
Nathaniel Hawthorne	Ezra Pound
Ernest Hemingway	Marcel Proust
Hermann Hesse	Ellery Queen
Victor Hugo	Ayn Rand
Aldous Huxley	Erich Maria Remarque
Washington Irving	Bertrand Russell
Henry James	J.D. Salinger
William James	George Sand
James Joyce	Carl Sandburg
Franz Kafka	William Saroyan
M.M. Kaye	Jean Paul Sartre
John Keats	George Bernard Shaw
Rudyard Kipling	Percy Bysshe Shelley
Arthur Koestler	Upton Sinclair
D.H. Lawrence	Aleksandr I. Solzhenitsyn
Jack London	Gertrude Stein
H.W. Longfellow	Robert Louis Stevenson
James Russell Lowell	Dylan Thomas
Thomas Mann	James Thurber
W. Somerset Maugham	J.R.R. Tolkien
Herman Melville	Leo Tolstoy
H.L. Mencken	Ivan Turgenev
Henry Miller	Mark Twain
H.H. Munro (Saki)	Robert Penn Warren

Evelyn Waugh

H.G. Wells

Walt Whitman

Oscar Wilde

Thornton Wilder

Tennessee Williams

P.G. Wodehouse

Thomas Wolfe

Virginia Woolf

William Wordsworth

William Butler Yeats

Emile Zola

Some "pretty great" contemporary authors

Edward Albee

Isaac Asimov

James Baldwin

John Barth

Saul Bellow

T. Coraghessan Boyle

Anthony Burgess

Truman Capote

John Cheever

Don DeLillo

Pete Dexter

E. L. Doctorow

J.P. Donleavy

William Gaddis

William Golding

Dashiell Hammett

Robert Heinlein

Joseph Heller

Lillian Hellman

John Hersey

Oscar Hijuelos

Jerzy Kozinski

Malcolm Lowry

Norman Mailer

Bernard Malamud

Gabriel Garcia Marquez

Cormac McCarthy

Carson McCullers

Toni Morrison

Joyce Carol Oates

Flannery O'Connor

Thomas Pynchon

Philip Roth

Isaac Bashevis Singer

Jane Smiley

Wallace Stegner

Rex Stout

William Styron

Anne Tyler

John Updike

Alice Walker

Eudora Welty

Some "great" works

The Adventures of
 Huckleberry Finn

The Aeneid

Aesop's Fables

The Age of Innocence

The Alexandra Quartet

Alice in Wonderland

All the King's Men

All Quiet on the Western Front

An American Tragedy

Animal Farm

Anna Karenina

Arrowsmith

As I Lay Dying

Atlas Shrugged

Babbitt

The Bell Jar

Beloved

Beowulf

The Bonfire of the Vanities

Brave New World

The Brothers Karamazov

The Canterbury Tales

Catch-22

The Catcher in the Rye

A Clockwork Orange

Confessions of an English
 Opium Eater

The Confessions of Nat Turner

The Count of Monte Cristo

Crime and Punishment

David Copperfield

Death Comes for the
 Archbishop

Death of a Salesman

The Deerslayer

Demian

Don Juan

Don Quixote

Ethan Fromme

Far from the Maddening
 Crowd

A Farewell to Arms

The Federalist Papers

The Fixer

For Whom the Bell Tolls

The Foundation

From Here to Eternity

The Ginger Man

The Good Earth

The Grapes of Wrath

Gravity's Rainbow

The Great Gatsby

Gulliver's Travels

Hamlet

Heart of Darkness

Henderson the Rain King

The Hound of the Baskervilles

I, Claudius

The Idiot

The Iliad

The Immortalist

The Invisible Man

Jane Eyre

JR

Julius Caesar

Kim

King Lear

Lady Chatterley's Lover

"Leaves of Grass"

The Legend of Sleepy Hollow

Les Miserables

A Long Day's Journey into Night

Look Homeward, Angel

Lord Jim

Lord of the Flies

The Lord of the Rings

MacBeth

The Magic Mountain

Main Street

Man and Superman

The Merchant of Venice

The Metamorphosis

Moby Dick

The Naked & the Dead

Native Son

1984

Of Human Bondage

Of Mice and Men

The Old Man and the Sea

Oliver Twist

One Flew Over the Cuckoo's Nest

The Optimist's Daughter

Othello

Our Town

Paradise Lost

The Pickwick Papers

The Picture of Dorian Gray

A Portrait of the Artist as a Young Man

Portrait of a Lady

Pride and Prejudice

The Prophet

Ragtime

"The Raven"

The Red Badge of Courage

The Remembrance of Things Past

The Return of the Native

"The Road Not Taken"

Robinson Crusoe

Romeo and Juliet

The Scarlet Letter

Siddhartha

Silas Marner

Sister Carrie

Slaughterhouse Five

Sons and Lovers

Sophie's Choice

The Sound and the Fury

Steppenwolf

A Streetcar Named Desire

The Sun Also Rises

The Tale of Genji

A Tale of Two Cities

Tender Is the Night

The Thin Red Line

The Time Machine

A Thousand Acres

Tom Jones

The Trial

Ulysses

U.S.A. (trilogy)

Vanity Fair

Walden

War and Peace

"The Wasteland"

The Way of All Flesh

Winesburg, Ohio

Wuthering Heights

Reading every one of these books will undoubtedly make you a better reader; it will certainly make you more well-read. The added bonus to establishing such a reading program is an appreciation of certain authors, books, cultural events, and the like that separates the cultured from the merely educated and the undereducated.

Read on and enjoy!

CHAPTER 12

Reading: A Lifelong Activity

> And further, by these, my son, be admonished: of making many books there is no end...
>
> —Solomon (Ecclesiastes 12:12)

 **W**ELL, YOU MADE it through another book. I hope you found the motivation—whether intrinsic or extrinsic—to define your purpose, discern the important details, grasp the main idea, and retain what you read. I promised not to preach about the joys of reading. And I haven't...too much.

Your need to read—and comprehend and retain what you read—will not end when you graduate from school.

Planning on working? From the very first week, when you're given the employee handbook, you'll be expected to seek out the facts—like what happens if you're late more than twice.

You'll be required to read critically—and know what statements such as "Our dress code requires professional attire at all times" mean.

Business proposals, annual reports, patient charts, corporate profiles, product reports, sales reports, budget proposals, business plans, resumes, complaint letters, inter-office memos—no matter what type of work you do, you won't be able to avoid the avalanche of paper and required reading that accompanies it.

Not only will your job require the ability to read and comprehend, but so will other facets of your life. If you plan to own your home, wait until you see the pile of paperwork you'll have to wade through.

Credit card applications? Better read the fine print to make sure you know when your payment must be in...and how much interest you're paying on that brand-new TV.

Insurance policies, appliance warranties, local ordinances, newspapers, membership applications, and tax forms—it seems like any goal you pursue in your life will require you to scale mountains of reading material.

For your own best interests, you must be prepared to read—and understand.

I wish you the greatest possible success in your future reading pursuits, of which there will be many...throughout your life.

Index